Scrapbook Fundamentals
Your Guide to Getting Started

From the Editors of Memory Makers Books, Denver, Colorado

Managing Editor MaryJo Regier

Art Director Nick Nyffeler

Contributing Editor Darlene D'Agostino

Photographer Ken Trujillo

Art Acquisitions Editor Janetta Abucejo Wieneke

Craft Editor Jodi Amidei

Graphic Designers Jordan Kinney, Robin Rozum

Contributing Photographers Camillo DiLizia, Jennifer Reeves

Photo Stylist Kevin Hardiek

Administrative Assistant Karen Cain

Editorial Support Amy Glander, Emily Curry Hitchingham

Contributing Writer Torrey Scott

Copy Editor Dena Twinem

Production Coordinator Matthew Wagner

Contributing Memory Makers Masters Amber Baley, Jennifer Bourgeault, Susan Cyrus, Kelly Goree, Kelli Noto, Suzy Plantamura, Valerie Salmon, Torrey Scott, Jessica Sprague, Danielle Thompson, Susan Weinroth, Angelia Wigginton

Published by Memory Makers Books, an imprint of F+W Publications, Inc.

12365 Huron Street, Suite 500, Denver, CO 80234

Phone (800) 254-9124

First edition. Printed in the United States.

10 09 08 07 06 5 4 3 2 1

Library of Congress Cataloging-in-Publication Data

Scrapbook fundamentals : your guide to getting started.
  p. cm.
 ISBN-13: 978-1-892127-81-5
 ISBN-10: 1-892127-81-4
  1. Photograph albums. 2. Photographs--Conversation and restoration. 3. Scrapbooks.
 I. Memory Makers Books.

TR501.S36 2006
745.593--dc22

2006044446

Distributed to trade and art markets by
F+W Publications, Inc.
4700 East Galbraith Road,
Cincinnati, OH 45236
Phone (800) 289-0963

Distributed in Canada by
Fraser Direct
100 Armstrong Avenue
Georgetown, ON, Canada L7G 5S4
Tel: (905) 877-4411

Distributed in the U.K. and Europe by
David & Charles
Brunel House, Newton Abbot,
Devon, TQ12 4PU, England
Tel: (+44) 1626 323200,
Fax: (+44) 1626 323319
E-mail: mail@davidandcharles.co.uk

Distributed in Australia by
Capricorn Link
P.O. Box 704, S. Windsor NSW, 2756
Australia
Tel: (02) 4577-3555

Memory Makers Books is the home of *Memory Makers*, the scrapbook magazine dedicated to educating and inspiring scrapbookers.
To subscribe, or for more information, call (800) 366-6465. Visit us on the Internet at www.memorymakersmagazine.com.

dedicated to u

...the new kid on the block!

Welcome to the fun and sweetly rewarding hobby of scrapbooking,
with all best wishes for a giddy, memory-filled journey!

Table of contents

Start this fun-filled adventure with ease by taming your photos and memorabilia with these simple suggestions for sorting, organizing and storing.

Discover all you need to know about the tools and supplies you'll see in the stores—for informed and budget-savvy purchasing.

Learn everything about the page-making process—from photo and paper selection to basic design principles—to help you create amazing scrapbook pages from the very start.

Introduction

What happens when scrapbooking becomes a part of your life? Your love of scrapbooking becomes a lifestyle, which forever changes the way you look at photographs and memories—and even the world around you! But like any new hobby, simply getting started can be the hardest part. In *Scrapbook Fundamentals*, we've mapped out everything you need to know to begin your adventure in scrapbooking.

This fun and rewarding journey begins with an enjoyable trip down memory lane as you organize your photographs and memorabilia to prepare them for scrapbooking. Then you'll take a pleasant romp through the maze of scrapbooking tools and supplies to better understand their use and your needs, followed by a delightful side trip into the basics of design principles to help you make your first scrapbook page with ease. From there, you'll discover the joys of journaling to breathe life into the stories behind your photos, then navigate your way through the creation of your first scrapbook album. Finally, you'll explore the various ways to connect with others who share a passion for scrapbooking.

In short, we put all the information and inspiration you need at your fingertips to help you begin your memory odyssey while encouraging you to see your world for what it is and love, preserve and enjoy every bit of it.

MaryJo Regier

Managing Editor

Memory Makers Books

1

Organizing Photographs & Memorabilia

A finished scrapbook is the ultimate destination—in it exists your beautiful and artistic collection of treasured photos and priceless memorabilia. But before that destination can be reached, a journey of organization must be undertaken.

Organizing a life's worth of memories will take time, dedication and patience. There will be moments of cringing (yes, you really did wear that). But, the greater the challenge, the sweeter the reward, and what could be sweeter than scrapbooking efficiency? Moreover, unorganized photos left in drawers and boxes are prone to get lost or, worse—destroyed.

To accomplish this task, all you need is one weekend's worth of time. Then, you should figure out a system that works for you. This chapter offers two: Sort chronologically or by theme. Once you decide on a system, you can begin to summit this seemingly insurmountable pile of photos in a few logical steps.

Sorting a lifetime of photos

Here is a golden opportunity to stroll down Memory Lane. Memory Lane is a long, meandering road—be sure to find a space in your home (out of direct sunlight) to accommodate its construction zone. Gather your photos, and start to sort them. Give yourself enough time to sit with your photos to let the memories wash over you. Don't be shy with the pen, either. Write down the details of a memory as they come to you.

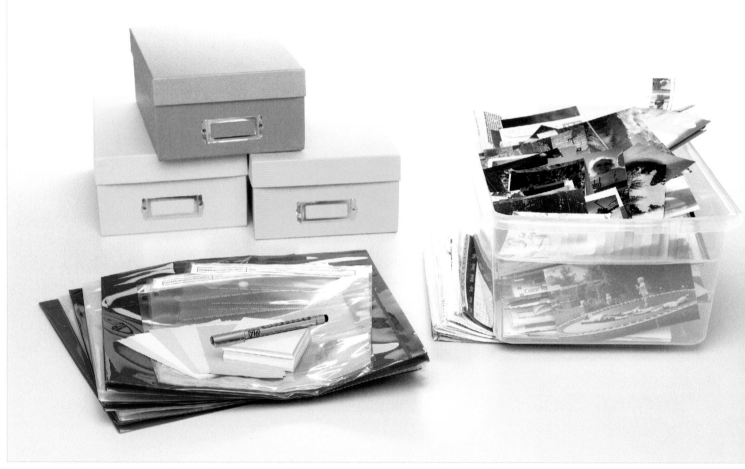

ORGANIZING PHOTOS

From mess to magical: Organizing your photos will be a rewarding experience. Bask in the memories, and dream of the scrapbook pages you will create to honor them. Rushing through this task will only make it a stressful one. Relax, and take it one photo at a time. Once you've finished, reward yourself with a trip to the scrapbook store.

What you'll need

- Index cards in several colors or archival-quality photo envelopes

- One or more large archival-quality photo storage boxes

- Negative holders if sorting negatives (see page 17) at the same time

- Black journaling pen

- Page protectors or a large box if sorting memorabilia at the same time

- Table or floor space that will allow you to leave materials out for a few days

- All of your loose photos

- Sticky notes for journaling

- Any old calendars on which you marked important dates and events (see pages 16-17 for information on safe photo storage)

- Follow the steps on the next page to begin organization

CREATING A CARD OR WORKSHEET FOR EACH YEAR

Create a worksheet or index card for each year of photos that you are sorting. Begin to sort photos into piles by year, placing them near the corresponding index card or worksheet.

NOTING MEMORIES TRIGGERED BY PHOTOS

Once your photos are sorted by year, grab any old calendars you have to help you further sort photos by month and event.

NOTING JOURNALING YOUR MEMORIES TRIGGER

Keep the sticky notes handy so you can jot down any memories that come to mind as you are sorting. Then, stick each note onto the back of the appropriate photo.

Sorting photos chronologically

Organizing photos by chronological order offers several benefits. It provides a straightforward organizational structure, and photos can be organized by theme within this structure. Follow these four simple steps, and photos will be organized in no time.

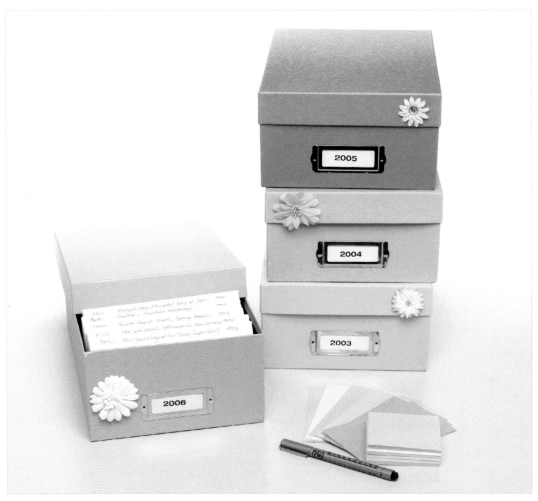

STARTING WITH THE CURRENT YEAR

Start with your most current photos. These photos hold the freshest memories, and recording them will help get you into the groove of organization. If the photos are still in their original envelopes with the negatives, transfer them to photo-safe envelopes (see page 17 for tips to organize and store negatives).

LABELING WITH DATES AND DETAILS

Label each envelope with a few details about the photos. Be sure to include the date(s) the photos were taken.

12

SORTING MEMORABILIA

If memorabilia accompanies the photos, make a notation on the photo envelope and store the memorabilia with the photos. Sort memorabilia by category such as "tickets," "journals" or "brochures." If you keep annual calendars or journals, file them with memorabilia.

SORTING ENVELOPES BY DATE AND FILE

Sort the envelopes by date and file accordingly. Place the labeled envelopes in chronological order in a photo-safe box.

Tips for sorting photos chronologically

- Gather all photos and memorabilia into one spot, out of direct sunlight.

- Start with the current year's photos. Separate the photos by month. Create a worksheet, if desired, to jot down notes about photos. Or, jot notes onto self-stick notes and stick to backs of photos.

- Once the photos are sorted by month, go back and sort by event or themes. Some common themes to sort by include wedding, vacation and holiday.

- Decide how you will store your photos—boxes, accordion files or sleeves. Take stock of your organization needs, and purchase the supplies. Be certain that the plastics you use are PVC (polyvinyl chloride)-free (see page 132).

Sorting photos by theme

Will the majority of your scrapbook albums revolve around specific themes, such as family vacations, holidays, daily life, school days or your wedding? If the answer is "yes," then it would be wise to sort your photos accordingly. Grab a few archival-quality boxes for photos and memorabilia, some photo-safe envelopes, a journaling pen and self-stick notes and start with one theme at a time.

NOTING THEME CATEGORIES

First, decide which theme you'd like to tackle first. Find a wide-open space in your home away from direct sunlight. Now, gather all your photos and memorabilia pertinent to that theme. Self-stick notes in hand, begin jotting down categories appropriate for that theme. For example, if you are sorting wedding photos, your categories could include The Proposal, The Engagement, The Planning, The Dress, etc. For a holiday album, you could designate the separate holidays such as Easter, Christmas and the Fourth of July as categories. In this example, photos from a vacation are organized by categories.

SORTING PHOTOS INTO THEME CATEGORIES

Begin to sort your photos into their respective categories. Be sure to spread out the self-stick notes so you'll have plenty of room to work. Try arranging the piles in a semicircle around you to lessen straining and reaching as you sort. Also, jot down names, dates, locations and details important to these memories to store with the photos.

RE-SORTING PHOTOS INTO CHRONOLOGICAL ORDER

Once your photos are sorted by category, organize each separate pile into chronological order. Think about the order in which you'd like your photos to appear in your album, and use that order to guide you. Place your tidy, sorted piles of photos into photo-safe envelopes and then into archival-quality boxes. Store them until you are ready to scrapbook.

Common themes for sorting photos

As you're sorting through a lifetime of photos, you may find major themes or categories begin to emerge naturally that would come together nicely for theme albums. Below are some of the major themes you may find in your photos. See page 106 for additional theme/category ideas.

- All About Me/You/Us
- Anniversary
- Baby
- Birthdays
- Celebrations
- Daily/Family Life
- Friends
- Heritage
- Holidays
- School
- Seasons
- Sports
- Vacation
- Visitors
- Wedding
- Your Home/Town

Storing photos and negatives

Once your photos and memorabilia have been organized, your next priority is storage. Your precious memories need to be kept in a safe environment, or your organization efforts will have been in vain. According to the Library of Congress, humidity is enemy No. 1. Ideal photo-storage humidity is between 20 to 50 percent. Consistent temperature also is important. Ideal conditions are 60 to 75 degrees Fahrenheit. Photos also should be kept away from bright, sunny exposure. Finally, keep photos and memorabilia away from rooms that experience a lot of chemical interchange (i.e., your kitchen). Think of storage like this: Would you want to live in your attic, basement, or anywhere else in your home prone to moisture, chemicals and fluctuating temperatures? Neither would your photos and memorabilia.

STORING PHOTOS

Invest in archival-quality photo boxes such as these in which to store your photos, negatives and memorabilia. These are materials that are acid- and lignin-free, and they have a pH level between 7.5 to 8.5. Avoid unsafe plastics as well. Look for plastics that are specially labeled for archival storage and photo use. These products are PVC-free and are made with polypropylene or polyethylene. Store photos upright in your archival-quality containers to avoid pressure damage.

STORING ADVANTIX FILM

Handling of Advantix and Polaroid films require a few extra considerations. Advantix films, specially made for Advanced Photo System (APS) cameras, come in a unique elliptical film cassette. When storing Advantix film, exposed or unexposed, keep it inside its cassette or canister in a cool, dry place. Advantix negatives never leave their canisters. Purchase special organizer boxes to store these. Never disassemble the Advantix negative cassette. Store cassettes with their corresponding index prints and label both for easy identification.

STORING POLAROIDS

Polaroid peel-apart prints are safe to cut for cropping. Do not use adhesives with Polaroids because they can chemically react with the backing of the photo. On scrapbook pages, place Polaroids in photo corners or inside memorabilia sleeves or pockets.

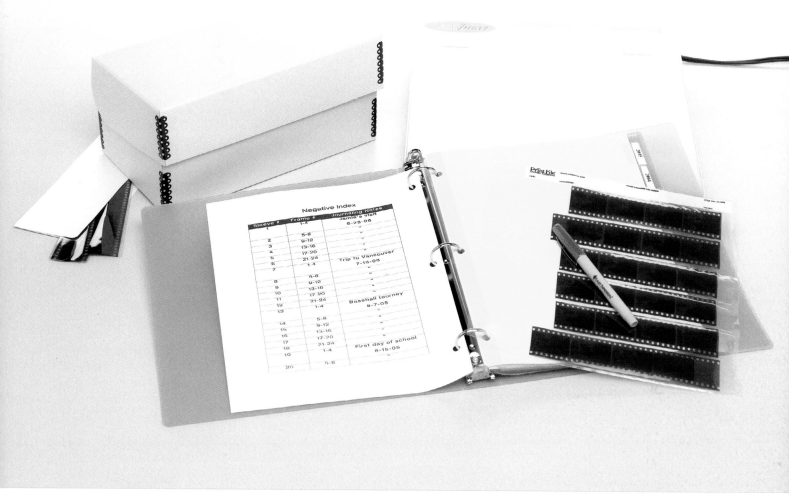

STORING NEGATIVES

Store negatives separately from photos for two reasons. First, in case of disaster, there's a better chance all of your memories won't be lost. Some scrapbookers keep their negatives in a completely separate location such as a relative's house for exactly this reason. Second, chemical reactions can occur between the two mediums.

Check your local scrapbook retail store or camera store for archival storage systems. Binders or boxes work great for negatives. Sort your negatives in the same fashion as you sort your photos. For a binder system, you simply need a three-ring notebook, archival negative sleeves and your negatives. Label the sleeves with the event, date

and people in the photos and be consistent. Create tabs for your binder with months and years. Include an index sheet in the binder to list the photos. Label the binders on the spine for quick reference.

If you choose to store negatives in a box, purchase acid- and lignin-free paper strips or negative pockets that are a bit larger than the negatives. Label the strips of paper and pockets with requisite data about the negatives. Separate negative strips with acid-free strips of paper to prevent them from sticking together. Label the box with full dates and add an index sheet of dates and events related to each box of negatives.

HANDLING AND CLEANING NEGATIVES

Handle your negatives as little as possible. Store them in similar environmental conditions for storing photos, but on the cooler side, if possible, and with 30 percent or less humidity. When working with negatives, wash and dry your hands thoroughly and keep them clean throughout the task. Be sure your work surface is dust-free. Wear white cotton gloves and hold negatives on outer edges only. Never cut negative strips. Clean dirty negative strips with a negative-cleaning solution such as PEC-12, made by Photographic Solutions and available in select camera stores or online (see Source Guide on page 139).

Organizing and storing memorabilia

Memorabilia, also known as ephemera, is the perfect accompaniment to your photos. The locks of hair, invitations, cards, ticket stubs, sports patches, newspaper clippings and more enliven the tale of your memories. With care, organization and proper storage, your precious mementos will be just as accessible for your scrapbooks as your photos.

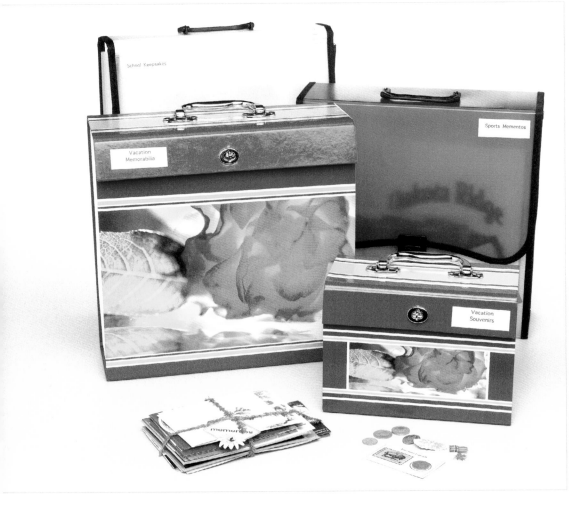

STORING MEMORABILIA

Memorabilia should be stored in conditions similar to those recommended for photo storage (see pages 16-17). Often, memorabilia itself is not archival and is prone to rapid deterioration. It is up to you to preserve it. Spray paper documents with acid-neutralizing spray, which will halt the acidic decomposition. The spray is available at many scrapbook retail stores and camera stores. Make backup copies of irreplaceable documents onto archival paper. Store everything in archival boxes, page protectors, accordion files, bags, albums or binders.

OVERSIZED MEMORABILIA

When memorabilia is too large to fit into your scrapbook, consider photographing it and including the image on a scrapbook page. Whether you hang on to the original is up to you. This is a great idea for school projects, trophies, uniforms and bulky homemade items.

Tips for photographing oversized memorabilia

- For outdoor shots, use 200-speed film and flash; shoot in open shade or soft sunlight.

- For indoor shots, use 400-speed film and flash; shoot in well-lit location or late in the day for a nostalgic effect.

- Arrange items on floor or table-top in an eye-pleasing display.

- Fill the frame with your arrangement when you look through the camera's viewfinder.

- Get as close as possible to accurately record words and numbers.

- Snap many photos from different angles, rearranging memorabilia as needed for visual appeal.

ORGANIZING MEMORABILIA SO IT'S READY FOR SCRAPBOOKING

Sort and organize your memorabilia while you sort and organize your photos. If you keep the organization system consistent between the two, it will seem logical and make things easier when it comes time to scrapbook. Number boxes, page protectors or pockets of memorabilia and then label boxes and envelopes of photos with the corresponding numbers. Create an index sheet for each container of memorabilia to attach to the respective storage container.

Make a copy of the index to file with the corresponding photos.

Store newspaper clippings separately from non-newsprint documents. Newspaper is highly acidic and could contaminate other documents. Treat it with acid-neutralizing spray and store in page protectors or memorabilia keepers. When adding to a scrapbook page, encapsulate it in a memory keeper or customized page protector to prevent cross contamination.

DE-ACIDIFYING MEMORABILIA

Before adding paper memorabilia to a scrapbook page, de-acidify it with a spray such as EK Success' Archival Mist. Another option: Color photocopy the documents onto acid-free paper.

ENCAPSULATING MEMORABILIA

Completely encapsulate memorabilia comprised of particulates or sharp edges in PVC-free (polyvinylchloride) memory keepers, available at scrapbook retail stores, to prevent photo scratches and damage to facing album pages. These containers also work great for small and loose memorabilia such as coins and lockets of hair.

Photo duplication methods

Picture this: You need a duplicate of a photo, but do not have the negative from which to create a reprint. What do you do? Take a deep breath, relax and consider any of these options. They are wonderful solutions for duplicating heritage photos or priceless prints that have become separated from their negatives.

TAKE A PICTURE OF A PICTURE

This method is great because not only does it result in a duplicate photo, you also wind up with a new negative. With a manual SLR camera outfitted with a close-up or macro lens, take a photo of the photo. Place your original photo on a flat surface or tape to a wall, focus and snap away in bright, even light for best results.

DIGITAL PHOTO MACHINE

Next time you're at your local discount, photography, drug store or supermarket, look for a digital photo machine (shown is Kodak's Picture Maker). These easy-to-use machines offer a variety of features, including size adjustment, custom cropping, rotating, zoom, sharpening tools and color and brightness adjustment. Some also allow the conversion of color photos to sepia or black-and-white prints. The machines create photo duplicates from prints, CDs or directly from digital camera media cards.

SCANNERS

Create your own digital darkroom with the help of your computer, scanner and printer. To reproduce a high-quality image, you will need to save the digital image as a high-resolution TIFF file, a quality scanner with the appropriate scanning software, a photo printer and high-quality photo paper. If you do not have the right equipment, you can ask a photo finisher to create high-quality scans of a photo to burn to a CD, which you can then print at home. Or, simply ask the finisher to scan and print the photos for you and give you a CD with the burned images.

PHOTO RESTORATION

As technology advances and scrapbookers become savvy users of image-editing software, at-home photo restoration is a possibility. But, for severely scratched, faded, and stuck-together photos, it's best to leave the work to a professional. When taking your photos to a professional, ask for work samples. Also, be sure to get a cost estimate. Restoration can cost up to $35 per hour. Remember, an ounce of prevention is worth a pound of cure—keep your photos stored in the proper conditions to prevent the need for restoration (see pages 16 and 17).

DAMAGED PHOTO

RESTORED PHOTO

Organizing and storing digital images

Digital images require just as tidy an organization system as tangible prints. Without one, digital files can be lost in the digital abyss. Once there, these files are impossible to find, and they eat up valuable hard-drive space. A good image-labeling system will ensure you can find just the image you need when you need it.

PHOTO-CD STORAGE

If CD storage towers and boxes do not appeal to you, CD binders are a great space-efficient storage option. Burn images to a disk, create an index print and slide both the disk and index into a slot in the binder.

IMAGE-LABELING SYSTEM

Create a labeling system that will be easy for not only you, but for others to understand and find images on your photo CDs. Keep it fairly simple, with just the right amount of information, to eliminate any guesswork when looking for one specific image. Additional tips are at right.

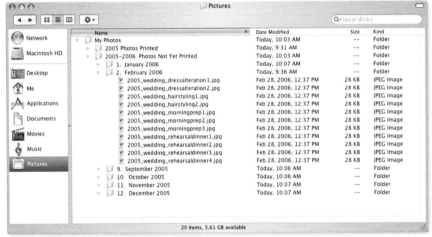

Organized digital photos
can happen in three steps

1 Choose a software storage program (chances are, a program was included with your digital camera).

2 Delete unwanted images as you take photos or when you download images to your computer from your camera. This is by far one of the greatest advantages to digital cameras; don't let it go to waste. Complete any image editing as you download, or create a folder to keep images in need of editing, and visit it on a regular basis.

3 Create a naming system. Be consistent with this step. Begin by labeling photos with the year. Next specify the event and add a topic (example: 2005_wedding_rehearsaldinner1.jpg).

MINI PRINTER

If you're a digital photographer on the go, consider purchasing a mini photo printer (shown is the Epson PictureMate). These purse-size printers will print 4 x 6" color prints straight from your media card, allowing you to clear space for more images.

Further, if you're a die-hard digital photographer, an extra external hard drive can be used for digital photo storage. This is a very efficient option for storing a large number of photos.

BURNING AND SHARING IMAGES

Burning images to a CD is the most common and easiest way to store digital images. It's also inexpensive. Store disks in jewel cases, binders or other containers that will prevent the disks from getting scratched. Online photo processing and sharing companies also offer photo storage with password-protected access. Do a Google search or try www.shutterfly.com for starters. The added benefit of this option is that friends and family can be given access to view the images, which they can then purchase for themselves.

2

Learning About Tools & Supplies

Scrapbooking, as an artistic endeavor, satisfies the creative spirit. But that's only half the fun. There is another side of scrapbooking that feeds another kind of spirit...the shopping side! Scrapbooking tools and supplies are so prevalent that entire stores are dedicated to them. Or, merge onto the information superhighway to effortlessly zoom from retail site to retail site, filling up virtual shopping carts with adhesives, albums, die cuts, pens, punches, stamps, stickers, templates and more. So much more that, in fact, your head starts to spin.

It's easy for both experienced and newbie scrapbookers to lose control when visiting the local hobby or scrapbook store or when shopping for goods online. Sometimes, intimidation can set in because there is just so much to choose from! With a little planning and by understanding your personal needs, you can be a successful and even economical shopper.

This chapter will guide you through the tools of the scrapbook trade. It will give you the information you need to make informed purchasing decisions. Also included are tips for organizing these supplies, how to care for them, and a few fun ideas for using them.

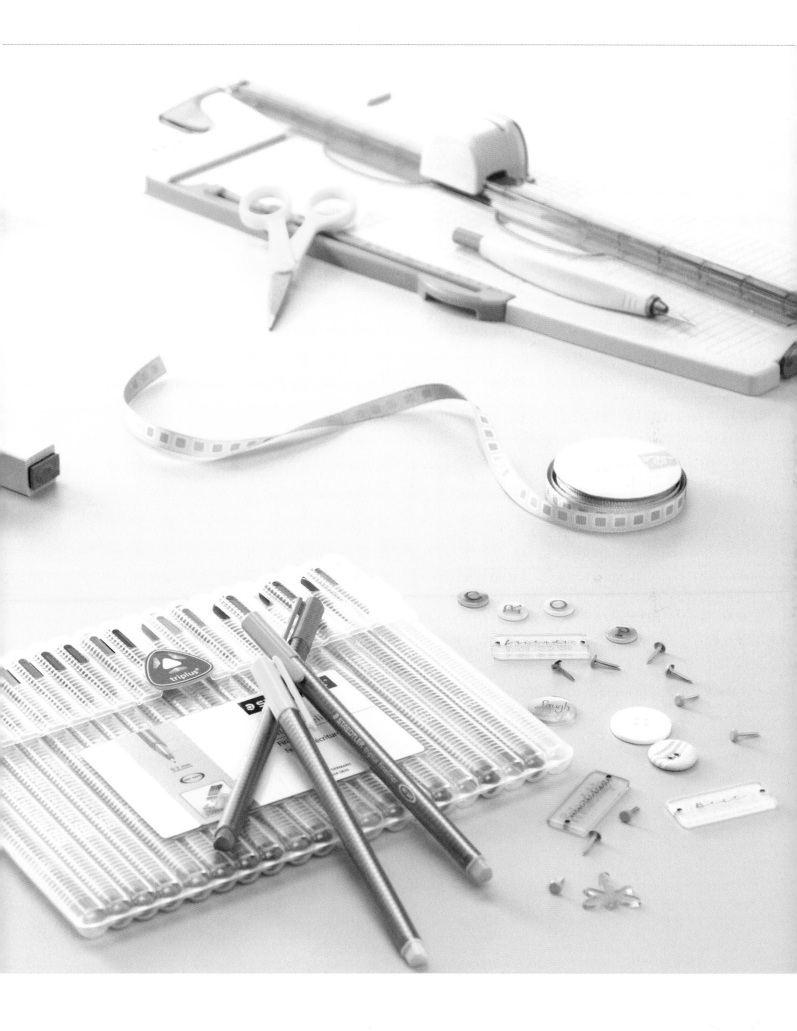

The basic toolbox

A few key tools will get you started scrapbooking. Chances are, some of the necessary tools are hibernating in your utility or junk drawer (see page 27). The other tools will require a small investment, but they will prove worthy. These are the tools that you will turn to again and again in your scrapbooking.

CONSUMABLE VS. NON-CONSUMABLE SUPPLIES

In scrapbooking, tools and supplies can be divided into two categories: consumable and non-consumable. Consumable tools and supplies are those that get used and will need to be replenished over time, such as cardstock or adhesives. Your non-consumable tools are trusty companions that, with proper care, will last indefinitely.

Consumable

 Adhesive remover

 Die cuts

 Ink pads

 Photo-safe adhesives

 Pigment pens and markers

 Solid and patterned papers

 Stickers

Non-consumable

 Craft knife

 Cutting mat (self-healing mats are recommended)

 Paper trimmer

 Punches

 Rulers

 Scissors

 Shape cutters

 Stamps

Tools you may already have

If you are new to scrapbooking but not new to crafting, you probably already own some requisite tools and supplies. Before you start shopping for your starter set of tools, nose around the house for a few basic items.

DO YOU ALREADY OWN THESE TOOLS?

Below is a list of tools that might already exist in your supply stash. Check this list before going shopping to prevent duplicate purchases.

OTHER TOOLS TO CONSIDER

As you progress as a scrapbooker, you will challenge yourself with new artistic techniques. Here are some tools that will help you grow as an artist.

Own these?

- Adhesive remover
- Craft knife and extra blades
- Cutting mat
- Metal straightedge graphing ruler
- Photo-safe adhesives
- Removable artist's tape
- Small, sharp scissors
- Tweezers

Other tools

- Colorants
- Decorative rulers
- Decorative scissors
- Paper crimper
- Templates

Using your tools and supplies

Wait! Before you reach for your wallet, even before you create a shopping list, spend some time learning about basic scrapbooking supplies. This easy education process will help you make the best purchasing decisions for your personal scrapbooking. If you learn anything in the next several pages, learn this: All supplies that you purchase should be of archival quality and safe for use with your photos and memorabilia.

Albums

A great album is the foundation of your scrapbook. Today's scrapbooker enjoys a range of choices when it comes to albums. They are available in a variety of sizes, in a rainbow of colors, and in an endless selection of styles. Think of your scrapbook needs when selecting an album—will the contents of your scrapbook require a lot of room or do you wish to find an album that you can put together in one weekend? Make sure the album is of archival quality. Page protectors should be made of nonreactive PVC-free plastic, such as polypropylene.

REMOVING PHOTOS FROM OLD MAGNETIC ALBUMS
Magnetic photo albums—the old albums with self-adhesive pages and plastic overlays—were the norm for years. Unfortunately, they are a horrible environment for your photos, causing them to discolor, become brittle and deteriorate over time. To remove photos from magnetic albums, loosen photos by gingerly slipping a slender knife or dental floss beneath a photo's corner to loosen it. Gradually slide the knife or dental floss behind the photo to remove it. If photos are really stuck, enlist the help of archival adhesive remover. If the plastic overlay is stuck to your photos, consult a conservator.

Bindings

1 **Post-bound.** This album features post screws in the binding. Unscrew the post to add, remove or rearrange pages. Purchase post extenders to increase the girth of the spine to accommodate extra pages or pages with dimension. Most post-bound albums include a starter set of pages with refill pages and page protectors sold separately. Some post-bound albums bind the page protectors into the album's posts rather than the page.

2 **Strap-hinge.** Strap-hinge albums employ plastic straps that are woven through sturdy staples attached to pages or page protectors. The main benefit of these albums is that they lie flat when opened, and facing pages lie close together and hide the binding. This style allows users to add, remove and rearrange pages.

3 **Spiral-bound.** These albums are recommended for projects that are not ongoing and have a definite end, such as

gift or theme albums. You cannot add or rearrange pages in spiral albums because the pages are already bound to them (although, you can remove pages if necessary).

4 **Three-ring binder.** This album can be the most user-friendly. It is expandable to the width of its spine. Pages slide in and out of top-loading page protectors, which are mounted on the binder rings. The drawback is the wide gutter of space that exists between facing pages.

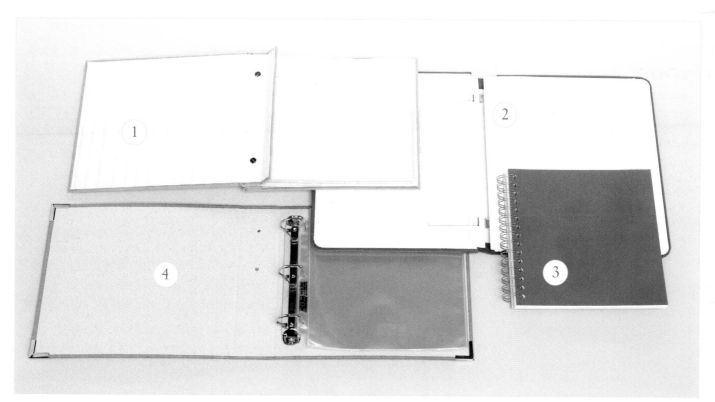

ALBUM BINDINGS

Choose an album with a binding style that complements your manner of scrapbooking. Some bindings make it easy to add pages anywhere throughout an album at any time. Other bindings don't allow you to add pages at all. Read to the right to help you find the right album.

Paper

Paper is essential to scrapbooking. In its most basic form, it provides a backdrop to your memories. But, because of its versatility and myriad specialty forms, it can be the one ingredient for elaborate accents. To be photo-safe, paper should be pH neutral (acid-free) and lignin-free. Buffered papers have alkaline substances added to prevent acids from forming in the future due to chemical reactions. Remember that not all specialty papers—such as vellum, mulberry, metallic, or handmade papers—are of archival quality. Don't let them touch photos and memorabilia.

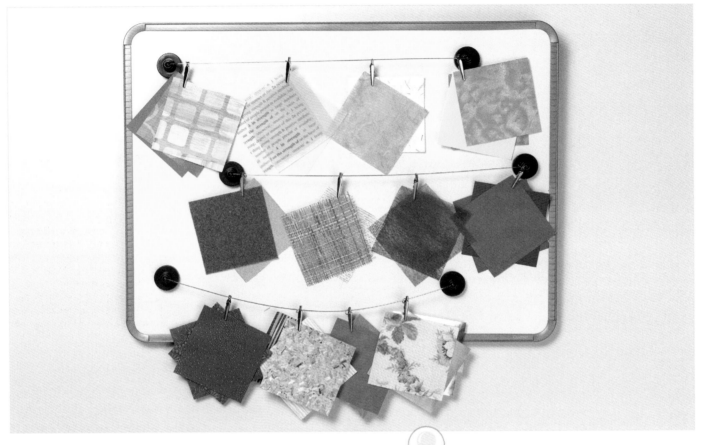

CARDSTOCK, PATTERNED AND SPECIALTY PAPERS

Acquaint yourself with the most common paper: cardstock. This sturdy paper is available in every color imaginable (and then some). It most commonly functions as the background for scrapbook pages as well as photo mats, but use it for any creative task that requires a solid color or stability. Next on the list is patterned paper. This multi-use paper is available in hundreds of designs and can unify pages with thematic patterns, colors and textures. Finally, there are specialty papers available—such as vellum and mulberry—which open up endless possibilities for page design and page accents.

Specialty papers

- **Vellum** is well-loved for its elegant and transparent quality. Draw on it, use it for computer-printed journaling or overlays, or print photos onto it for an airy effect.

- **Suede paper** has the appearance of brushed leather. The subtle texture works great for pages that call for rugged, rustic or fashionable touches.

- **Mulberry paper**, when torn, gives scrapbookers the highly-coveted look of feathered edges. It has an inherent botanical feel.

- **Handmade paper** lends a vintage or antique quality to pages. Many times elements are embedded within the rough strands that make it appropriate for festive (confetti), outdoorsy (botanical) or heritage (soft fibers) pages.

- **Metallic paper** can be industrial, rich or simply add a little pizazz. Some are even holographic. Metallic papers are available in a range of colors and are great for replicating metallic objects, such as jewelry, eyeglasses, picture frames, etc.

For the longest time, Olivia had some trouble relaxing for the camera (which really is strange considering she's had one stuck in her face since the minute she was born)! She would end up with more of a grimace than a smile which really frustrated me—I wanted her photo to be as stunning as the girl I was eyeing up in the viewfinder! Lately however, she's been a real natural when I go to take a shot, and I've been absolutely stunned with the results! She's always been a beauty to me but now we have the documentation to prove it. We all have to find our comfort level in front of the lens (I'm still working on it), but as for Olivia, she's got it!

Patterned-paper page

Choosing patterned papers that go together can be confusing and intimidating, especially for new scrapbookers. Renee shows how easy it is to put patterns together like a pro. Her secret? She uses patterned papers from the same design line. Most manufacturers design entire lines of coordinating papers and page embellishments to take the guesswork out of choosing what goes with what.

Renee Foss,
Seven Fields, Pennsylvania

ORGANIZING AND STORING PAPER

Some scrapbookers have a million sheets of paper; others have only a few. All need to store paper in a manner that keeps it clean, dry and away from direct sunlight. Storage towers are a great option because they allow you to see your supply stock and utilize vertical space for organization efficiency. Try sturdy, archival-quality files for smaller paper collections; these are also handy for cropping on-the-go. Keep solid-colored paper sorted by "ROYGBIV" (red, orange, yellow, green, blue, indigo, violet) rainbow order. Sort and group patterned papers by design theme. Keep specialty papers that may not be of archival quality separate.

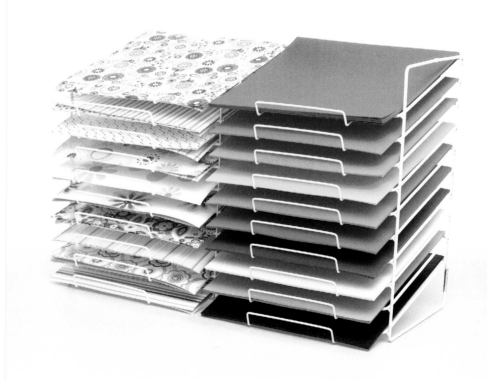

31

Dry adhesives

The selection of scrapbooking adhesives can overwhelm a beginner, but relax. Choosing the right adhesive rests on two decisions—personal preference and whether or not you need a dry or wet adhesive. Dry adhesives do not require drying time, but the bond may not be as strong as the one created from a wet adhesive. Below are some common uses for dry adhesives. Be sure all of the adhesives you use, especially those for adhering photos, are archival quality.

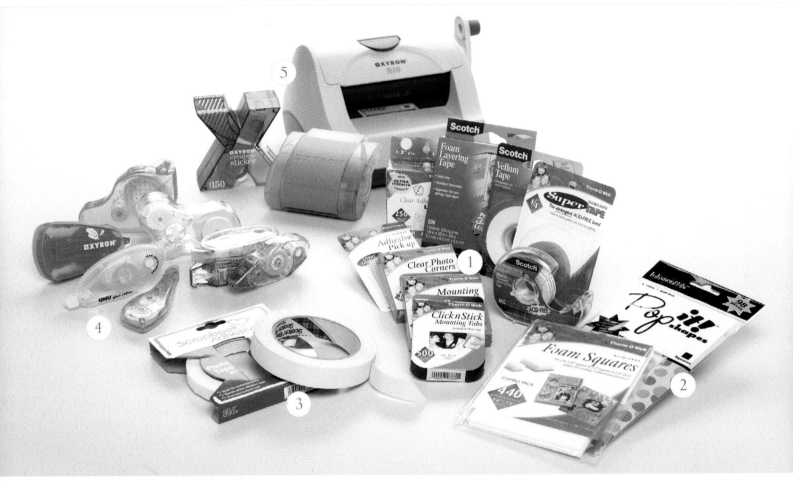

MOUNTING PHOTOS

Always use dry adhesives to attach photos to your pages. They are stable and provide all the bonding you need. Also, they are easy to use and less messy.

Types of dry adhesives and their uses

1 **Photo splits.** This is double-sided tape precut into tiny squares. These are great for creating photo mosaics, adhering titles and journaling blocks and paper embellishments to pages.

2 **Foam adhesive.** When you want dimension, you want foam adhesive. This double-sided tape comes in a variety of sizes and thicknesses.

3 **Photo tape.** Also double-sided tape, this adhesive is packaged on a roll. It is not pre-sectioned; scrapbookers cut the tape into necessary lengths. This works great for larger photos and lightweight embellishments.

4 **Tape roller.** This applicator dispenses double-sided adhesive as you roll it across a surface. This is the most versatile of all dry adhesives.

5 **Xyron adhesive-application machine.** Run photos or paper accents through this machine to transform them into stickers. This machine is great for adding adhesive to anything transparent, such as vellum.

Wet adhesives

Wet adhesives produce a stronger bond, but also need time to dry and set. Plus, they require tidy execution. If you need to use a heavy-duty wet adhesive, read the label carefully to be sure it is of archival quality. If you are unsure, do not allow photos or memorabilia to come into contact with it. As an extra precaution, mat photos and memorabilia with buffered paper for projects such as these.

ADHERING PAGE ACCENTS

Wet adhesives come in many varieties. Consult the productpackaging label if you are not sure which adhesive to use or what its intended purpose is. Also, experiment with different types to see which you like best.

Types of wet adhesives and their uses

1 **Bottled glue.** Use this with photos if the project requires a strong bond. Be careful when applying; using too much can cause paper to buckle. This adhesive works best with small embellishments and dimensional objects such as sequins.

2 **Glue sticks.** This is the happy medium between wet and dry adhesives. Inside a glue stick exists pastelike adhesive that dries quickly. It also dries flat. Glue sticks are great to use with large photos and blocks of paper as well as die cuts.

3 **Liquid glue pens.** When you need an adhesive for small details, reach for a glue pen. When pressed against paper, these pens dispense small amounts of liquid glue.

Cutting tools

If one tool will make scrapbooking easier, it's the right cutting tool. Cutting tools crop photos, cut photo mats, create borders, trim edges, and more. Every scrapbooker should own a pair of large and small straightedge scissors for general-purpose cutting. With just a little confidence, scrapbookers can master all types of new techniques by experimenting with the wealth of exceptional cutting tools on the market.

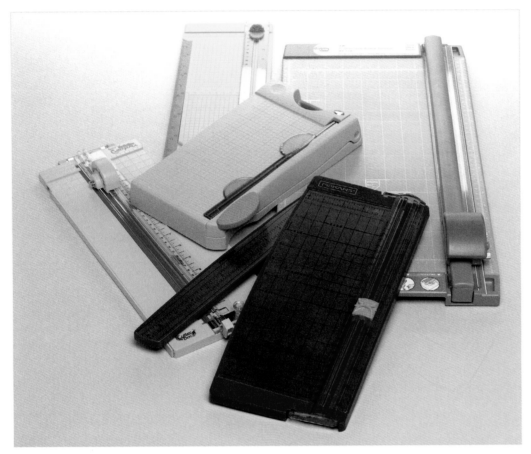

PAPER TRIMMERS

Paper trimmers cut straight edges and 90-degree angles. They come in several sizes. Smaller trimmers work great to cut mats or cleanly crop photos. Larger trimmers, such as a rotary-disc trimmer, handle longer cuts and are necessary for cutting through thicker materials, such as heavyweight cardstock and corrugated paper.

USING A PAPER TRIMMER FOR STRAIGHT CUTS

Position desired paper or photo under cutting guide of trimmer, making certain to squarely butt paper against lip of upper edge of trimmer. To ensure square cuts, start with blade at bottom of guide. Grasp cutting blade and using gentle downward pressure on the blade, push blade in track toward upper edge of trimmer to complete cut.

CRAFT KNIVES

Craft knives, perhaps the tiniest of all cutters, require the most skill. Begin by using the craft knife for straight cuts. Use with a cork-backed metal-edged ruler. Or, use a craft knife to reach into tiny spaces. For best results, always be sure the blade is sharp. Also, when not in use, keep the blade covered (craft knives are apt to roll off tabletops) and always keep away from children.

DECORATIVE SCISSORS

Whether you crave shallow and sharp edges or soft and flowing, decorative scissors come in an endless variety of patterns and depths of cut. When using decorative scissors to cut fancy edges, try flipping over either your scissors or your paper and cut again to create mirror images of the same design. You can also combine different scissors in various cuts to create a multitude of designs.

USING DECORATIVE SCISSORS FOR PATTERNS

To use, draw a guide on your paper where you plan to cut. Line up the blade slightly to the left of the penciled line. Steady your arm by anchoring your cutting elbow on the table and use your other hand to turn the paper as you cut. Make long, steady cuts. For an even pattern, carefully realign the blade after each cut.

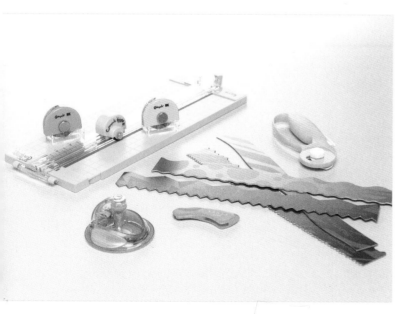

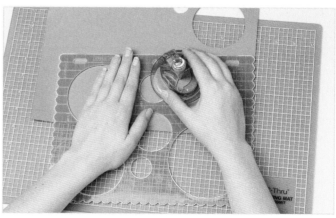

SHAPE CUTTERS

Shape cutters will help you create perfect shapes. Use them for cutting photo mats, journaling blocks or to cut geometric shapes for paper accents and background patterns.

USING SHAPE CUTTERS TO CREATE UNIQUE CUTS

On cutting mat, place shape template on paper. Position cutting blade against inside edge of shape of template. Hold cutter as directed by manufacturer and move smoothly around template to create cutout shape, applying even pressure until you have completed the revolution.

Miscellaneous tools

In scrapbooking, the crafting possibilities are infinite. Shown here are a few tools that will help make your life as a scrapbooker easier and more productive. Keep them handy, as you'll want to use them quite frequently.

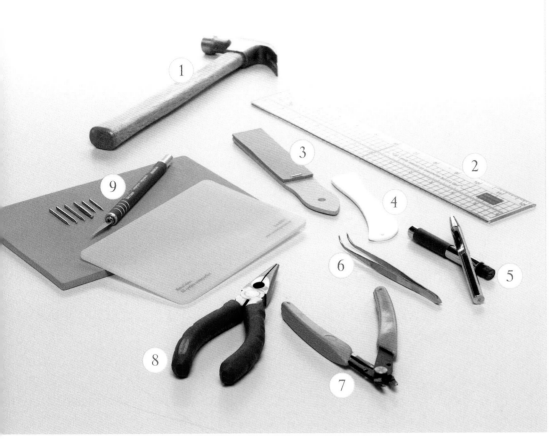

Additional tools for your supply box

As you pioneer your own scrapbooking trail, your tool needs will grow based on your crafting preferences. Some tools you may wish to add to your scrapbooking toolbox are:

1 hammer

2 graphing and/or metal straightedge ruler

3 sandpaper

4 bone folder

5 eyelet-setting tools

6 tweezers

7 button-shank remover

8 needle-nose pliers

9 interchangeable craft knife and paper-piercing tool

REMOVING BUTTON SHANKS

Buttons are wonderful scrapbook page accents because they add light-weight charm, can support a page theme, and come in an endless variety of styles and colors. But, to lay flat, they need to have their shanks removed. On backside of button, snip button shank from button front using button shank remover in similar fashion to wire cutters or scissors.

SETTING EYELETS

Eyelets can be both decorative and/or useful and are easily applied or "set." To set an eyelet, punch a small hole in the desired location of the paper. Insert eyelet and flip over the paper. Press setting tool into center of eyelet and firmly pound top with hammer.

Pens

Before you get excited about pen possibilities in your scrapbook, be sure that any pen you use is a pigment pen. Pigment ink is lightfast, fade-resistant, waterproof and colorfast. Pens are useful for not only writing captions and journaling, but also for adding detail work, such as faux-stitching marks or squiggly borders. Practice with your pens—correct usage will add to a page while unexpected results can ruin one.

JOURNALING PENS

The pen-cap number signifies the pen-tip size. Pen tips range from very fine and delicate (lower numbers) to thick and dramatic (higher numbers). When journaling, take the time to find a pen that complements your own writing style. The pen should feel comfortable in your hand and allow you to write smoothly. If you are purchasing your first pen, opt for a basic black journaling pen. Once you find a tip you like, invest in others like it.

DECORATIVE PENS

Once you feel comfortable with journaling pens, expand your creativity with decorative pens. From brush to bullet and calligraphy to chisel, these pens come in a variety of tips, colors, opacities and even luster. Beginners should opt for a general-use bullet tip first and experiment from there. Decorative pen tips produce different results. Here's just a small sampling of what the various decorative-pen tips can create.

Pen-tip examples

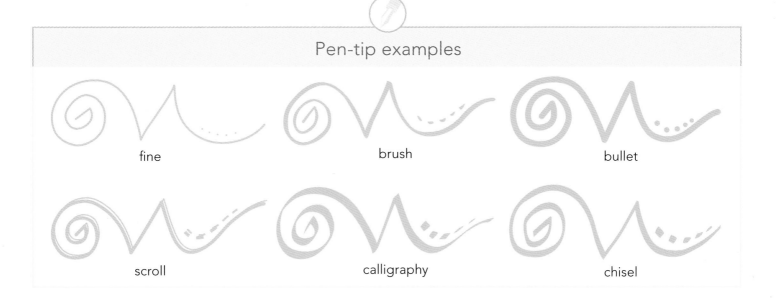

fine

brush

bullet

scroll

calligraphy

chisel

Templates

Templates are stencil-like patterns made of plastic, sturdy paper, or cardboard. You can create them yourself or purchase them. Basic shape and letter templates are wonderful investments for scrapbookers because of their varied uses.

TEMPLATE TYPES

Templates come in a variety of shapes, sizes and themes that include hearts, animals, simple geometrics, page borders and photo frames. Journaling templates also exist to help scrapbookers write on not only straight lines but swirling spirals. Letter templates come in a variety of sizes and styles, from chunky block-style lettering to miniscule calligraphy. Decorative rulers make decorative borders and pen detailing a snap.

Template page

Templates are a great aid in adding titles and shapes for embellishment to your layout. Valerie uses a letter template to customize a title for her layout from coordinating patterned papers. She also uses a template to create circle and flower shapes to decorate her page. When using a template, turn the template so the letters are backward and trace their outline onto the backside of your desired paper. By doing this, you won't have to worry about your guidelines showing on the finished product.

Valerie Salmon, Carmel, Indiana

Punches

Punch art ranges from simply chic to extremely elaborate. Beginners just need to insert paper, press the button, and pop out a perfectly punched shape. Since they are available in hundreds of sizes, shapes and designs, beginners should choose a versatile punch for an initial purchase. Simple shape punch sets are a wise purchase as are tag and letter punches.

USING OFFSET PUNCHING TO CREATE FRAMES

Turn your punch upside down to aid in positioning your paper for accurate punching. To create frames using nested punches, use smaller punch first to punch out middle of frame. Then align the larger punch around the punched negative space of smaller punch and depress punch to create a perfect frame.

PUNCH TYPES

Geometric and theme punches are easy-to-use tools for shaping photos and paper page accents. Corner-rounder punches can be used for rounding the corners of photos and photo mats. Hand-held punches work great for punching holes in handmade tags.

Punch page

A current trend in punches is the manufacturing of punches in graduated sizes. These "nested" punches lend themselves well to graphic-looking page accents. Linda not only used the punches to make decorative elements on her page, she also used them to punch out the support photos and create the mats for the photos.

Linda Harrison, Sarasota, Florida

Stickers

If you are looking for an easy way to spice up a scrapbook page, think stickers. Stickers are readily available in any size, theme, color, shape and style to add peel-and-stick spark to your projects. Avoid the dreaded "sticker sneeze" on your pages by using them selectively. If you are unhappy with your sticker placement, simply remove with a careful application of adhesive remover.

STICKER TYPES

Letters and numbers, borders and accents, even journaling blocks—there is a sticker to meet every scrapbook design need. Use the following tips when designing with stickers: Draw a guideline for letter and border sticker placement. Allow large stickers to stand on their own; group smaller stickers together. Combine stickers with other page elements, such as photos or die cuts. Accent titles with stickers. Create mini scenes with themed stickers. Use stickers to create page borders or to visually tie spreads together.

PAGE   PRODUCT

Sticker page

Stickers have definitely "come into their own" over the years. No longer are they only cutesy and cartoonish. Today's stickers are as sophisticated as they are varied. Amber uses an entire line of coordinating stickers to decorate her layout. From the letter stickers in her title to the tag and shape elements that adorn her layout, Amber combines them in perfect harmony on her page.

Amber Baley, Waupun, Wisconsin

Rub-ons

As scrapbooking grows, so does the love affair between scrapbookers and rub-ons. Rub-ons add quick detail to pages. They can be applied to any surface, even metal and plastic. Now they are available in countless styles and colors.

RUB-ON VARIETIES

Rub-on accents, when applied to a surface, create a seamless image. Rub-ons first romanced scrapbookers as lettering accents. Then came phrases and simple shapes. Now, full-color images and entire rub-on overlays are available to use on layouts much like a printed transparency. Sheets of rub-on color also are available to use with your own handwriting or for creating resist images and more. Place the rub-on image in the desired location and brandish to the surface with a dull-edged object, such as a wooden craft stick, bone folder or spoon.

PAGE	PRODUCT

Rub-on page

You can achieve the look of computer-manipulated photos and page elements by using rub-ons like Janet does on her fresh and cheery layout featuring rub-on letters on the photo and a rub-on dot pattern on the word "you." Use rub-ons to create titles, enhance journaling or add playful decorative elements to your layout.

Janet Hopkins, Frisco, Texas

Die cuts

Die cuts are precut shapes that come in both printed and solid colors. They are wonderful themed accents. Purchase them individually or by the pack, or cut your own using your local scrapbook store's die-cutting machine for a small fee. Be sure the die cuts you purchase and the ones you create yourself are made from acid- and lignin-free paper.

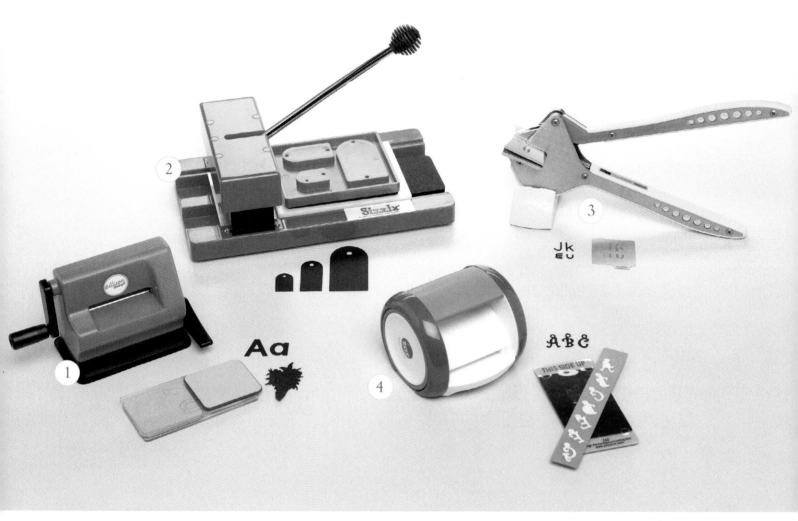

DIE-CUT MACHINES

For years, die-cut machines were large and expensive. Now, several manufacturers are making it possible for crafters to own personal die-cutting systems. Some machines are created with portability in mind, while others aim to be all-in-one machines capable of embossing and stenciling as well as die cutting.

Die-cut machine options

1 **Ellison Tag-a-Long:** use hand crank to roll dies through to make shapes

2 **Sizzix:** dies are placed face down on paper; shapes are cut by pressing down on the handle

3 **QuicKutz Squeeze:** die is inserted into magnetic head; pressing down on handles makes the shape

4 **AccuCut Zaz:** rolling action activates die-cutting blades

Die-cut page

Die cuts have come a long way over the years. Today's die-cut shapes are sophisticated and come in thousands of designs. By using white-core cardstock, Torrey dresses up her die cuts by gently sanding them to bring out the details. From letters to shapes and decorative elements, die cuts are a fun way to jazz up your layout in a snap.

Torrey Scott, Thornton, Colorado

MAKING DIE-CUT SHAPES

Personal die-cutting machines rely either on hand pressure or a rolling mechanism to produce a cut. In this case, place paper on cutting mat of die-cut machine. Position die on paper, foam side toward paper. Slide assemblage to rest under press. Lower handle completely. Advance assemblage as needed to complete cut.

Stamps

Stamps are a one-way ticket to impressive results in little time. Basic stamping is very simple, and you'll be surprised at the beauty of the results. Stamps are available in every theme, size and shape imaginable. Start off with a few pattern stamps or a set of simple geometrics. A set of mini lettering stamps is also a wise investment that will help make titles and journaling a snap.

STAMP VARIETIES

Hundreds, if not thousands, of varieties of stamps are available. There are see-through acrylic, wooden rubber and foam stamps. Lettering stamps are great—oversized lettering stamps are available in unique styles for page pizazz. Pattern and texture stamps are easy ways to add lightweight dimension and interest to pages.

Stamped page

When it comes to scrapbooking, stamps are one of the most versatile tools you can own. Angelia easily creates a customized background using multiple stamped images of flowering branches. With stamps, you can craft tailored accents, titles and even journaling to perfectly match your layout.

Angelia Wigginton,
Belmont, Mississippi

STAMPING HOW-TO

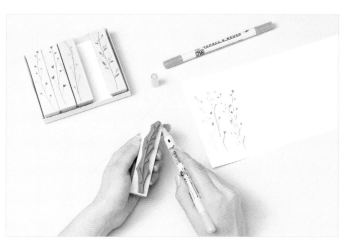

INKING A STAMP

Press stamp directly onto inkpad, making certain entire image surface of stamp is evenly inked.

COLORING A STAMP

An alternate method of inking a stamp is to directly apply ink to the stamp using dye-based felt marker. Multiple colors can be used with this technique. Simply color the image surface of the stamp with the desired color(s) of marker. Once inked, gently exhale directly on the stamp surface to reactivate the ink before stamping.

CREATING A STAMPED IMAGE

On flat, solid work surface, firmly press inked stamp onto desired paper to ensure a complete image transfer. Pigment ink takes longer to dry but is preferable because of its colorfastness as compared to dye ink. Drying time can be shortened by holding stamped paper near a heat source for several minutes.

Colorants

Beyond basic pens, markers and inkpads exist a range of colorants that can add vibrant accents to any scrapbook page. Each colorant has its own distinctive characteristics and unique properties, which impacts its use, care and organization needs.

COLORANT TYPES

If you are new to colorants, begin with any of the following: chalk, colored pencils, inkpads and tinted clear gloss medium. They are no-fail ways to add color to pages. Chalk is great for edging torn paper and adding dimension. Colored pencils can be used with stamps and to add shading and definition. Using inkpads directly on paper will result in the popular distressed look. Tinted clear gloss can be applied over paper accents for shiny subtle color.

Colorants

1 Watercolor pencils

2 3-D crystal lacquer and chalk enhancer

3 Solvent and instant-dry pigment inkpads

4 Fluid chalk and pigment inkpads

5 Crystal-color lacquers

6 Blending chalks

7 Glitter chalks

APPLYING CHALK

Gingerly applied chalk will define torn edges, enhance the texture of paper or embossed designs and add subtle shading and dimension to all sorts of page accents that have a rough or porous surface. Chalk can be applied with a cotton swab, makeup sponge or your finger. Experiment on scrap paper and always set with a fixative spray. Gently rub foam applicator, sponge or cotton swab on surface of chalk. Apply chalk using circular rubbing motion to torn paper edges, die cuts, punched shapes or other page elements to create depth and added interest.

COLORANT HOW-TO

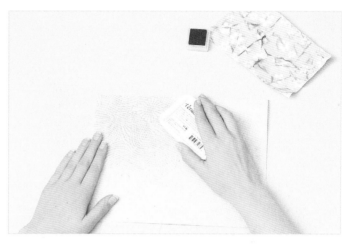

USING WATERCOLOR PENCILS

Colored pencils are the easiest colorant to use. Chances are you know how to use a pencil, and cleanup simply requires that you collect the pencils and put them away in their proper place. Most brands of colored pencils are considered to be acid-free. Using a random crosshatch pattern not only adds color, it also adds texture to page elements.

STAMPING BACKGROUNDS

Add definition to the raised surfaces of embossed papers or the peaks of crumpled paper by lightly running an inkpad across the top. Highlight the texture and dimension of embossed or crumpled paper by inking the surface of the paper using gentle rubbing motions over paper surface.

APPLYING INKED DEFINITION

By rubbing an inkpad directly onto the edges of your paper, you create instant definition. Invest in basic black and brown pigment inkpads. Gently scrape inkpad directly onto edge of paper to create a softly worn, finished look. This method of applying ink is called direct-to-paper (DTP) inking.

ADDING LACQUER SHINE

Add dimension and shine to sticker and other page embellishments. Apply stickers to paper as desired. Accent stickers or other elements by applying coat of clear lacquer. For more dimension, apply several coats of lacquer, allowing each coat to dry thoroughly between applications. If bubbles appear, use edge of paper piece or toothpick to gently pop unwanted bubbles. Allow to dry 24 hours.

Embellishments

Embellishments are to a scrapbook page what accessories are to a fashionable outfit. They provide just the right detail—they don't overwhelm, nor are they so understated that they become invisible. After selecting the photos and writing the journaling, many scrapbookers enjoy the hunt for the perfect embellishment. There are so many to choose from—it's not hard to feel like a kid in a candy store. During the hunt, opt for embellishments that enhance your page theme in regard to subject, size, color, texture and mood.

EMBELLISHMENT VARIETIES

From handmade to handpicked, there is an embellishment for every occasion. Today's scrapbooking accents can be found in a variety of textures and materials. Popular looks include space-age acrylics, flexible and fun rubber, modern plastic and versatile metal. Pages also can be accented with fiber, thread, ribbon, jute and twine. Of course, buttons, beads and baubles will always be popular choices.

Embellishments

1 Ribbons

2 Beads and baubles

3 Acrylics and buttons

4 Threads and fibers

5 Organics

6 Metallics

WINNER

Oct. 2005

Katelyn, I was so impressed with your SEARCH class's project this year: the Butterfly Migration Play. You made such a darling Gulfstream Butterfly with your dark orange wings. And I was extremely impressed with how you learned your lines all by yourself. I never hear about these things unless I'm invited to see you in action, and I'm so glad you invited me! I was thrilled to hear that your team won a national recognition award. How fun that the ceremony was held in Orlando, Florida, because that meant we got to go. Just you and me! I'm so proud of all of your accomplishments. You are an amazing girl!

Embellished page

Embellishments give our layouts flavor and texture. Without embellishments our pages would seem flat and lifeless. Jennifer used a combination of ribbons, acrylic letters, paper flowers and metal accents to bring her layout to its beautiful finish.

Jennifer S. Gallacher, Savannah, Georgia

EMBELLISHMENT HOW-TO

ATTACHING METALLICS

Metal can be masculine, feminine, futuristic or vintage. In fact, metal can be tailored to meet the needs of any page theme. When using flat metal on your page, choose an adhesive strong enough to keep it secure. For brad fasteners, pierce guide hole on front of paper using piercing tool or large needle. Push ends of brad through hole and splay apart on back of paper to secure.

ATTACHING RIBBON

Ribbon and fibers are easy to use and add awesome detail to pages. A quick idea for ribbon is to staple folded lengths to create a frilly border. Use both ribbon and fibers as tag toppers. Or set two rows of eyelets or brads and lace or wind ribbon/fiber around them. In this example, adhere ribbon to layout by rolling an adhesive-tape runner down entire length of ribbon on backside. Fold ends to back of layout and adhere to add finished look.

ATTACHING ACRYLICS

Durable, lightweight, transparent acrylics wowed scrapbookers a few years ago and have ever since. Acrylic accents can be found in the shape of letters, geometrics and themed creations. They are a good choice for those who crave lightweight dimension. Most often, they come in carefree styles, so use them for playful and spirited designs. Apply glue dot to back of acrylic accent by pressing back of accent firmly on glue dot. Gently pull glue dot and acrylic accent from backing and affix element to layout.

ATTACHING OTHER ACCENTS

Beads, baubles, flowers and other page accents will add glitz and glam to elegant, sassy or sophisticated pages. Be sure to use clear-drying adhesive or a strong double-sided tape when adhering them to your page. In this example, press silk flower, bead or other embellishment directly onto glue dot and gently lift element and glue dot from backing. Affix to layout as desired. If glue dots are unavailable, use a small spot of liquid glue as adhesive.

Premade page accents and page kits

For quick class, opt for premade page accents. Accents range in styles from simple and sophisticated to ornate and whimsical. Most also are self-adhesive, so you don't need to worry about how to attach them to a layout.

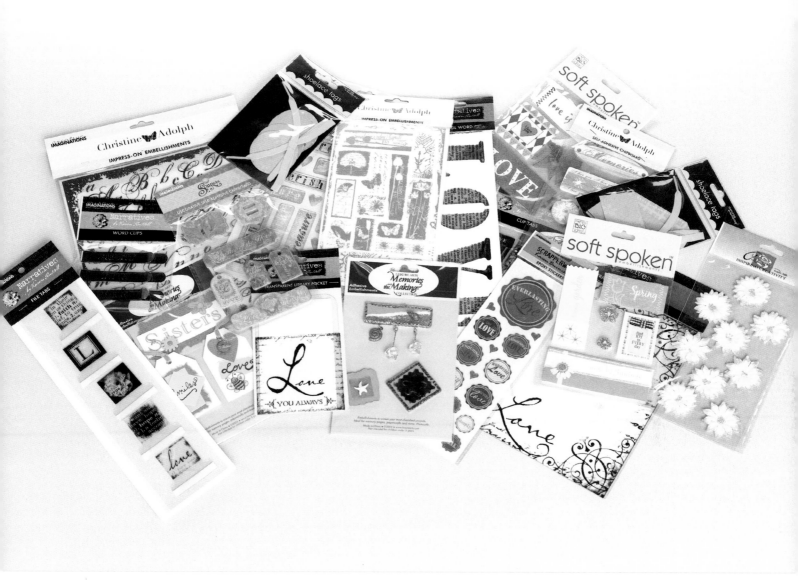

PREMADE PAGE ACCENTS

Several manufacturers offer pre-made page accents for today's busy scrapbooker. The accents often look handmade, which gives a layout an instant wow factor. Also, premade page accents are often part of coordinating product lines, making it easy for scrapbookers to effortlessly match papers and accents to photographs.

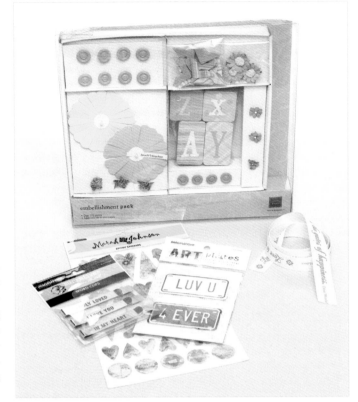

PAGE ACCENT KITS

More and more product manufacturers are now producing page accent kits, complete with letters for titles and coordinating page accents. They help make scrapbooking quick and easy by eliminating the guesswork of mixing and matching page accents that visually go well together.

PAGE   PRODUCT

Embellished page

Not only do scrapbooking manufacturers realize that we may not have the time and energy to make our own embellishments, they recognize that we still crave excellence and detail when it comes to decorative elements for our pages. By choosing many premade embellishments to use on her layout, Heather creates a detailed and elegant layout in no time flat.

Heather Preckel,
Swannanoa, North Carolina

Store-bought page kits

Page kits are a one-stop shop for scrapbookers. Inside a page kit is everything a scrapbooker needs (except photos and journaling) to create a few pages or even an entire theme album. The product matches perfectly, so the scrapbooker saves time trying to coordinate them. Also, many page kits include layout ideas, which saves time if you are struggling with design inspiration.

PREMADE PAGE KITS

For the beginning scrapbooker, a page kit makes the hobby less intimidating. It includes all of the product you need as well as layout ideas. For the intermediate to advanced scrapbooker, a page kit saves you time shopping for product so you can focus on creative scrapbooking techniques to personalize the pages.

3

Designing Your First Scrapbook Page

The photos have been organized. The memories have been noted and detailed and stowed with the organized photos. You've excitedly put together your scrapbooking toolbox, cleared space in your home office for your creative endeavor and you're ready to begin. But...where do you start?

First, stop thinking of a blank page as, well, a blank page. Start thinking of it as a playground for your creativity. On your creative playground, there is no right or wrong. There is only the unique reflection of you. As you grow as a scrapbooker, you will develop a style.

This chapter is a hand-holding guide to creating a layout. As you are introduced to basic design concepts, you also will learn how to choose an engaging focal photo, how to successfully pick and mix papers, how to use color and more. As you learn these skills, notice how they are used in other scrapbook layouts. Let these layouts inspire your creativity and encourage you to experiment.

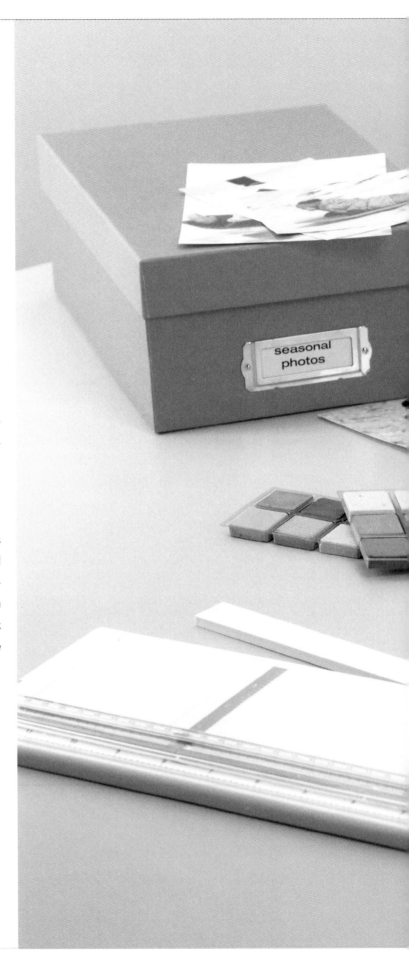

The page-making process

A few simple steps—that's all it takes to create a scrapbook page. If you approach page creation logically, you will develop a creative process. Over time, your creative process will help you evolve into a well-oiled scrapbooking machine. Here is a simple overview of the page-making process. The following pages will examine it further.

1. SELECT PHOTOS

The first step in creating a scrapbook page is photo selection. Choose the most engaging, telling photos for each spread. Consider the mood and intent of the page, and select photos to match.

2. DETERMINE FOCAL PHOTO

When selecting photos, choose the most expressive as the focal photo and use the rest as support images. Pick only the photos that add important details to the page.

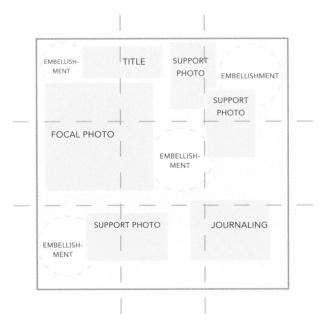

3. SELECT PAPERS

Color is one of the most influential design elements, and effective use of paper colors on a scrapbook page will transform it into a work of art. Pick papers with colors to reflect that mood of the page you have in mind.

4. CONSIDER LAYOUT AND DESIGN

A pleasing layout design will grab a reader's eye and guide it around the layout. Take some time to experiment with photo and accent placement. Consider the use of line quality—do you wish to have hard, straight edges with strong feelings or soft, curving lines that flow with subtle energy?

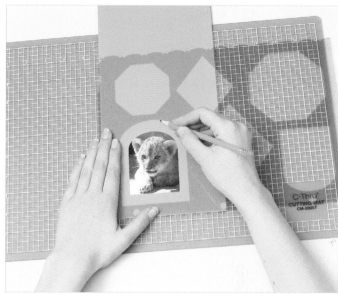

5. CROP PHOTOS

Crop photos either to remove distracting elements or to dramatize the image. Cropping will help focus the reader's eye on a distinct element of the image and remove anything extraneous.

6. MAT PHOTOS

A mat goes beneath the photo. It provides a buffer between the photo and any potentially unsafe elements on the scrapbook page. Effective matting also helps "pop" the photo off the page. Try using mats in colors, shapes and angles that contrast against the background for maximum effect.

7. ADD TITLE AND JOURNALING

No page is complete without a title and journaling. Use the title to alert the reader to the page subject. The journaling will fill in all the details. Be sure to include the "who, what, where, when and why" (and, sometimes, "how") in the journaling.

8. ADD PAGE ACCENTS

Finish your page with accents. Use accents that match the theme of the page in regard to subject, size, color, texture and style.

Photo selection

It's common for new scrapbookers to feel an obligation to use every single photo. While you can use as many photos as you wish, try not to feel guilty if you don't use them all. Strive for using the best photos—photos that have the most impact. Also, keep in mind that too many photos can overcrowd a page. As a rule of thumb, try to use three to five images per page. These photos should work well together and complement each other in terms of color, composition and content.

SELECTING THE BEST PHOTOS TO USE

The focal photo—it's the image that stops you in your tracks, the one you linger over. The expression of the photo subject speaks to the scrapbooker to say exactly what's on his or her mind. Draw attention to this photo by cropping out any distracting elements and enlarging it.

DETERMINING THE FOCAL PHOTO

Most professional photographers will tell you that, out of a 36-exposure roll of film, they are lucky to get one or two great shots. When choosing photos, spread them all out in front of you. Which ones make you smile or sigh? From those, group any that are similar and pick the best, or the ones that are most telling of the memory. Be sure your final selections include an assortment of close-up shots and photos that contain details of the memory.

Paper selection based on photographs

After the photos and journaling, paper is the most important scrapbooking element. It provides not only the foundation for your scrapbook page, but also helps develop the desired mood through colors, patterns and textures. Take some time to choose the perfect papers for your page.

CHOOSING PAPERS

Fan your photos out atop an array of papers to help determine which papers go best with them. These papers offer the perfect complement to these photos. At first glance, it might not appear so, but in terms of color, the papers convey the natural yet wild theme of the photos. The patterns bring a curious playfulness that enhances the theme of the zoo photos. Finally, the subtle colors and artsy designs of the papers match the intent of the artist add to a sense of unexpected excitement to the scrapbook page.

Designing with color

Color will make or break the mood of your scrapbook page. Color, after all, does affect our emotions. If you want to create a somber mood for your photos, don't head to the yellow section of the paper aisle. If you are new to working with color, start simple. Monochromatic color schemes consist of the varying shades of a single color. They are a classic choice. As you become more comfortable with using color, experiment with more unconventional choices.

HOW PAPER COLOR SETS MOOD

Color is the strongest mood alterer you can employ on a scrapbook page. Color theory supposes that color affects our moods and emotions. For example, red is associated with love, anger and elegance. Blue is associated with sadness, serenity and stability. Also, be aware of color temperatures. Warm colors, such as red, orange and yellow, will impart a cozier feeling than cool blues and greens.

USING A COLOR WHEEL

Let the color wheel guide you to perfect and even unexpected color selection. On it are divisions of primary (blue, red and yellow), secondary (green, violet and orange) and tertiary (mixtures of primary and secondary colors, such as blue-green) colors. Hold the wheel up to your photos to select a dominant color. Then experiment with different color combinations.

HOW PAPER HELPS SHOW CONTRAST

The right paper choice will make your photos "pop" off the page. When selecting papers, you want photos to contrast, not blend, with the background. When choosing papers, study your photos. First choose a background color that contrasts with the background of the photo and base accent colors off of that first choice.

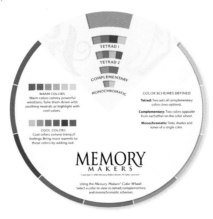

Designing with patterns

The patterns and colors of the papers you choose for a scrapbook page should be an extension of the story. Your scrapbook page captures a memory, and therefore the colors and patterns should also aptly and subtly reflect that memory. Look at your photos to choose colors that appropriately convey the tone of the photos. Then find textures that can be mimicked in patterned-paper designs.

MIXING PATTERNS

Mixing patterned paper designs will create a background with depth and interest. If you are new to mixing patterns, experiment with a simple mix of florals and geometrics. The organic shapes of the floral pattern will contrast cleanly with the linear quality of the geometric designs. For a successful mix, make sure the base color of the chosen patterned papers match (for example, don't mix paper with a white base with paper that has a cream base, or the result will look dirty).

MIXING PAPER-PATTERN SIZE AND SCALE

When mixing patterns, be aware of the scale of the printed motifs. A successful mix of patterned papers will feature a dominant, or larger, motif and smaller motifs of varying sizes and intensities. Otherwise, the mix will lack definition and overwhelm the eye. To begin, start with a mix of three patterns. Choose a dominant motif and two support motifs, one of which should be of a delicate design.

Learning about layout and design

Scrapbook page design is the visual expression of your memories. All the page elements, from the photos and journaling to the papers and layout, should speak in unison to convey the tone of the story that unfolds on the page. The next few pages will provide a strong foundation from which to build strong scrapbook pages.

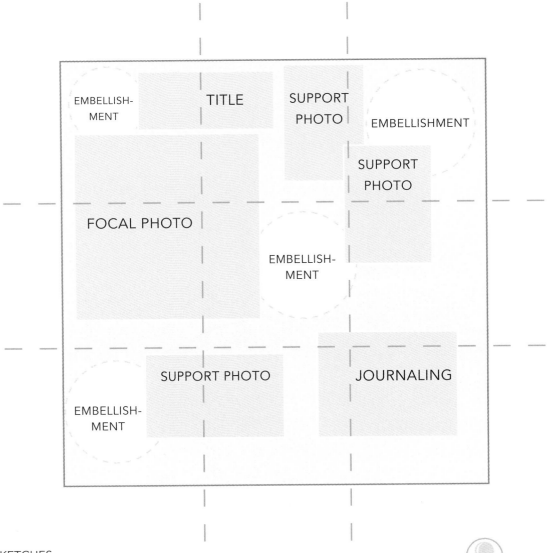

GRIDS OR SKETCHES

The next time you pick up a magazine, find an advertisement with a pleasing design. Study it. Chances are the design can be divided into blocks of information (for example, the title, the image, the text). Professional graphic designers create designs based on grids. Borrow this technique for designing scrapbook pages. Divide a page into three or four equal quadrants on which to place your blocks of information (the title, the photos, the journaling and page accents). The object of the game is to keep the grid balanced. Experiment by sketching layout ideas on grid paper.

Space for journaling

Most scrapbookers save the task of journaling until the very last. While there is no right or wrong way to create a scrapbook page, doing this can cause design problems. Try to have all of your page elements completed before you sit down to design your page. This will ensure proper design dimensions as well as room left over for journaling.

RULE OF THIRDS

Photos taken and layouts designed based on the "rule of thirds" most often lead to balanced and interesting images. Images and layouts composed using this rule can be divided into three equal spaces. To begin, mentally divide an image or layout you wish to photograph or design into nine equal quadrants (a grid of three rows and three columns). Place your subject or key elements on or near any of the intersecting points. For portraits, be sure the subject's eyes fall on or near an intersection.

SHAPE AND LINE

Shape is another important concept of design. When designing a scrapbook page, the quality of the lines and shapes within the design should speak to the mood of the layout. Line and shape can convey as much mood as color—think about the energy in strong diagonal lines and shapes with irregular and acute angles. Conversely, lines and shapes can show a gentler side with soft curves and flowing waves.

THREE TYPES OF SHAPES

When you think of the word "shape," chances are a square, rectangle or circle will spring to mind. But, those three common forms are simply one type of shape—geometrics. In design, there are three types of shapes: geometrics (structured shapes that create the foundation of a design), natural (plants, animals and people—use these to create a serene and fluid feel) and abstract (simplified versions of natural shapes—these can result in a modern feel). Use shapes to set a tone and to help guide the eye and organize your page design.

RULE OF THIRDS

Crop photos so that key elements of the subjects fall along thirds. Use placement of background papers, title and photos along the thirds of your layout space.

SHAPE AND LINE

Line refers to the physical placement of elements to create a visual path or "flow" of a layout. Arrange a title and support photos to create a visual line to guide the viewer's eye across and diagonally down a layout.

TYPES OF SHAPES

Cropping photos and papers into shapes can emphasize characteristics on the page. Shape your journaling to hug the profile of a photo.

FOCAL POINT

In scrapbooking, a focal point is usually a photo. Enlarging a photo, or changing it to sepia or black-and-white, will help it become the page's focal point. Matting photos in interesting ways is another way to create a focal point of your layout.

A View To The Underwater World

It isn't very often that the opportunity to view life from an underwater perspective presents itself. Kevin and Michael took full advantage of the situation and stood, transfixed, until they were pulled away.

SPACE

Sometimes it's not what you put on a layout that impacts the viewer, it's what you *don't* put on. Use white space effectively to give your photo or photos breathing room without making it look too stark.

FOCAL POINT

It's a necessity for every scrapbook page. It's the page element that the eye zeroes in on at first glance to provide a starting point for the viewer. Most often, the focal point is the most stunning and telling photo of the pack. But, it can also be a journaling block or other page element. The easiest way to emphasize a focal point is through size. Other ways to draw attention to a page element include creative framing or matting, changing the color of a photograph, grouping several photos together or positioning elements so that they direct the eye to the focal point. You can also create emphasis through repetition and contrast in line, shape, texture and color.

SPACE

The concept of "space" in design is important. Effective use of blank or unfilled space, called "white space," in a layout can be a strong design tool. Too much white space and your layout looks bare. Too little, and you end up with a cramped layout that is cluttered and confusing to the eye. Scrapbookers sometimes feel obligated to cover every inch of their layouts with something—whether it be photos, stickers or page accents. But sometimes less is more. Space is just as powerful a design element as shape, texture or color. Well-used space gives a layout breathing room, allowing the photo to shine on a simple background. Use space to prevent crowding of page elements. Tighten space when elements appear to be floating.

We could sit for hours watching the primates' antics. The big gorillas are so regal and intimidating while the orangutans are just plain silly. This particular day, the gorilla paced his enclosure and we tried to guess why he was so agitated. The orangutan sat right up against the window and flipped through a phonebook. We imagined he was looking for a good lawyer or perhaps a company that would be willing to deliver pizza to the zoo. . . .

PRIMATE HOUSE

RHYTHM

Rhythm is created by repetition and/or arrangement of page elements to create a cohesive look. Accomplish this by using repetitive touches of your background throughout a layout. Arrange supporting photos in a circular configuration to add an eye-catching rhythmic balance to the overall design.

BALANCE

Use a dark, prominent title to balance out an oversized focal photo. Without this element to add weight to the bottom of the layout, the page would seem very top-heavy. The grouping of support photos adds even more weight to the lower right side of the layout and also helps balance out the heavy upper left side.

RHYTHM

Rhythm in music is the repetition of beats. Rhythm in design is the repetition of elements. Just like a song moves your body to dance, a rhythmic design moves your eye about the scrapbook page. Create rhythm by repeating patterns, shapes, colors, page accents or photos. A photo series that shows an action in progress also will create rhythm. Keep in mind that rhythm does not require the repetition of identical elements, patterns, shapes and so on. Rhythmic variety will spice up a page design.

BALANCE

You may take the best photographs, write the best journaling, choose the best paper and accents, but none of it will matter if your page design is not balanced. For a page design to be balanced, individual page elements must be evenly distributed to complement one another. Balanced page designs can be symmetrical or asymmetrical, but they always share unity, flow and rhythm. When striving for a balanced design, consider the visual weight of objects. Darker, larger, bolder and more colorful page elements will be heavier than their lighter, smaller, more subtle and paler counterparts. Evaluate finished page designs by mentally dividing the page in half, both horizontally and vertically. Does each side balance the other or does one feel heavier?

SYMMETRY

If you favor structured, organized designs, symmetry will help you achieve that goal. Symmetrical pages are ones in which one side of the page is a mirror image of the other. The sides can be identical reflections or be reversed to create a true mirror image. Symmetrical designs require an even number of page elements (for example, two, four or six photos).

If you're more drawn to free-form designs, create asymmetrical layouts. While these are more challenging to balance, they are just as pleasing to the eye. Asymmetrical designs are not created from identical halves, and are normally constructed with an odd number of page elements. Choose one or the other based on the number of elements you wish to include.

UNITY

Unity in design means the sum of the individual parts equals a successful whole. In scrapbook design, it means the photos, journaling, and title work together to set a tone that in turn is supported by the layout's colors, textures, accents, line and shape quality, and layout structure. Unified designs have a definite flow. Evaluate your page designs and ask yourself if all of the pieces fit within the structure you've created. Does each piece aptly convey the desired mood? Does everything have an appropriate place?

SYMMETRY

To demonstrate the concept of symmetry, divide your background in half horizontally and employ a reverse-mirror effect by horizontally and then vertically flipping the arrangement of your photos and page elements.

UNITY

Create unity by repeating geometric elements (in this case, circular) found in the background and in many other elements on your page. The use of circles, in all sizes, throughout the layout effectively ties it all together.

Creating continuity on page spreads

Many scrapbook layouts consist of two side-by-side pages called a "spread." When designing a spread, it is best to consider both halves as one continuous page. This will result in a balanced and unified design. The two pages will read as one harmonious story that flows effortlessly and uninterrupted across the middle.

RULE OF THIRDS
A color-blocked background, title and photo-border placement follow this rule to ensure visual appeal across the spread.

BALANCE
Multiphoto borders are easily counterbalanced with a large and weighty title.

SYMMETRY
One design layout, rotated and repeated for second page, creates symmetry across the spread.

FOCAL POINT
Enlarged photos on both pages provide strong focal points. Photo subjects face one another to help draw viewer's eyes across the spread.

RHYTHM
Repeated design elements such as color, pattern and journaling strips on both pages tie everything together.

SPACE AND LINE
Same-sized support photos, in a linear configuration, make great use of space and line across a spread.

UNITY
The same background on both pages creates unity.

Creating continuity across a two-page layout

- **Use a border** A border that runs the length of both pages will visually connect the two. Run the border across the top and bottom of the spread or around all four sides.

- **Create a seamless background** The easiest way to do this is to simply use the same background paper for both sides of the spread. If you want to enhance the background with color- or pattern-blocking, stamping or another technique, be sure to build the background on both halves at the same time.

- **Coordinate colors** You want the completed halves of the spread to coordinate. Stretch color combinations across both halves for an ensemble look.

- **Create movement** Extend interactive elements, such as pop-ups, peekaboos and moving parts, across both halves of the spread.

- **Split photos or design elements** Connect spreads at the seam by running a panoramic scenery shot or enlarged photo across it.

- **Mirror a design** Mirror the layout design on each side of the spread. The design can be identical or reversed for an authentic mirror image. Keep the shapes and matting consistent.

- **Run a title across** Connect two sides of a spread by stretching title lettering across both halves. It will naturally guide the viewer's eye across both sides.

- **Allow contact** When photos touch, your eyes follow them along the sequence. Allow the photos to flow across the gutter of two pages.

- **Repeat an element** Carry a repeating element across both pages to create rhythm and natural eye movement between the halves of the spread. This can be achieved with a photo series, journaling captions, stickers or other page accents.

Cropping photos

Photo-cropping techniques encompass everything from removing distracting backgrounds to enlarging the focal point of an image or slicing and dicing photos to transform them into dramatic works of photo art. No matter how elaborate the technique, the goal is always the same: enhance the image.

ORIGINAL PHOTO

CROPPED, ENLARGED PHOTO

DROP, CROP AND FLOP

Professional photographers hope to get one or two awesome images from a roll of film. Identify the best photos for your layouts, using the "drop, crop and flop" philosophy. If there are two or three photos that are similar, pick the very best one and drop the others. Pick the best photo and emphasize it. If the subject is too small, show your photo processor where to crop the photo before enlarging it. If in your favorite photo the subject's eyes are facing off the page (which draws the viewer's eyes away from the page), your photo processor can flop the photo by reversing the negative before printing.

ENGAGING CLOSE-UP;
NO CROPPING NEEDED

CROPPING FOR VISUAL INTEREST

While background clutter in a focal photo can distract from the subject, background detail in support photos helps to tell the story. Layouts should have a mix of engaging close-ups and detail-rich support images. When cropping scenic photos, try not to put the horizon line in the middle of the frame. Let an interesting foreground fill two-thirds of the frame. If the sky is the most interesting part of the image, allow it to fill two-thirds of the frame. When cropping images of people, avoid cropping at joints (neck, elbow, wrist, hips, knee, ankle). Otherwise, images could make the viewer uneasy or feel disjointed.

REMOVE UNNECESSARY BACKGROUND;
TAKE PHOTO SUBJECT OFF-CENTER

Matting photos

A good mat will make a photo jump off a scrapbook page. Mats should complement the photo and contrast, not blend, with the background. Mats also provide a buffer between photos and elements that could chemically react with and potentially damage them.

USING A TEMPLATE TO MAKE A MAT

Use a template to crop a photo and to create a coordinating mat. Adhere cropped photo to cardstock. Align template over photo. Trace outline of shape onto cardstock. Using scissors or a craft knife, trim photo mat just inside guideline.

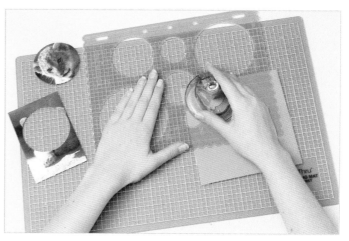

USING A SHAPE CUTTER TO CREATE A MAT

Shape cutters are also a great way to easiliy mat photos. On cutting mat, position shape template on photo. Start with cutting blade butted against inside edge of shape on template. Hold cutter as directed by manufacturer and move smoothly around template to cut photo into desired shape. Using slightly larger version of same shape, create a matching mat for your photo.

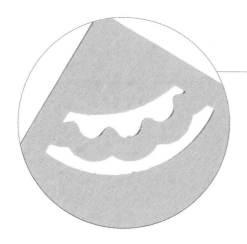

USING CORNER-SLOT PUNCHES TO DESIGN A MAT

Dress up a regular photo mat with decorative corner punches. These punches come in a variety of styles, including simple rounded corners and scalloped edges. Be sure to match the design of the punch to the mood of your page. Photos slip easily into the slotted edges. Turn punch upside down and insert mat squarely into punch. Failing to seat your mat squarely in punch will result in a ruined mat. Press punch firmly to create decorative slots in which to slide corner of photo. Repeat process on each of the four corners if desired.

Matting ideas

Contrast is the design key for creating custom mats that emphasize photos. There are a myriad of fun and unique ways to mat or frame your photos to add visual interest. The following ideas are sure to inspire unique matting techniques for your photos.

STITCHED MAT

Add zest to a photo by triple matting it on cardstock and randomly sewing around photo on the largest mat. Adhere a bow to corner of mat to hide the start/stop of the stitching.

RIBBON FRAME

Design a playful ribbon frame by mounting lengths of ribbon along photo edges, securing ribbon junctures with brad fasteners at photo corners.

RIBBON-WRAPPED FRAME

Wrap a photo with ribbon after it's been matted and mounted on torn cardstock. Add a button for visual interest.

DISTRESSED FRAME

Create an edgy white border without adding bulk by simply sanding the edges of the photo to remove emulsion.

SELF-FRAME AND MAT

Self-frame a photo by marking lines $\frac{1}{4}$" in from all four sides on back of photo. Cut on lines with a metal straightedge ruler and craft knife, cutting out center of photo. Trim $\frac{1}{8}$" off of two adjacent sides of photo. Mount both frame and center on cardstock.

TAG MAT

For a tag-shaped mat, mat photo with cardstock and adhere to patterned-paper background. Trim into a tag shape. Punch a hole at the top and tie with fibers.

Mounting page elements

Now it's time to put everything in its right place. You've lived the memories and taken the photos. You've transformed journaling notes into a lovely story. The focal photos have been cropped and enlarged and supported with accent images. The page supplies have been picked, and the chosen design and color support the mood. It's time to build your page by mounting all of the elements.

ASSEMBLING THE PAGE

As you begin to build your page, often you will mount the cropped and matted photos to the background first and attach the rest of the elements after. If you have sketched a page design, use it to guide you. If you are wary of committing to a page design, use temporary adhesive on the backs of the photos so you can experiment with their placement. Applying adhesive should be the last step after all elements have been placed on a layout. Starting with the background, adhere layout elements in desired position. This allows you to easily change your design as you go without running the risk of ruining a layout due to ripped paper from removing permanently adhered elements.

Adding a title

A title defines a page. It conveys a message to the viewer, alerting him or her to who or what the scrapbook page is about. It also is a design element. It helps unify a scrapbook page—as a design element a title can create balance; connect two halves of a double-page layout; promote the page theme through color, texture and shape; and create movement. Take time crafting a title that will grab a viewer and enchant him or her to relish a page.

CREATING LETTER-STICKER TITLES

Sticker letters are another fun and fast way to make a title for a layout. Use a ruler to aid in sticker placement to ensure your words are straight and evenly spaced. Some rulers, like the one shown, are designed to be used specifically for centering elements such as letters.

DESIGNING COMPUTER-PRINTED TITLES

Use your computer and printer to create a quick and easy title. With the availability of thousands of fonts and ink colors, you can create a perfect title in no time at all. Print title out on cardstock and mat with contrasting cardstock. Use a paper trimmer to create the size of photo mat you desire.

MAKING RUB-ON-LETTER TITLES

Titles are an important part of your layout. They should be an integral part of the overall design and not just put on as an afterthought. Using previously affixed page elements (such as photos) as guidelines assures your title not only fits in its allotted space but also is straight. After you have mounted the photos, add the title. If you are mounting individual letters, use a grid ruler to evenly space the letters.

Title ideas

Titles can be simply crafted or inspiring works of art. They can also be simply crafted to look like inspiring works of art. Below are four variations for one title treatment. Notice how each variation conveys a different mood or feeling. Experiment with your own tools and supplies to discover the endless possibilities you have at your fingertips for creating unique, one-of-a-kind page titles.

STAMPED TITLE

Stamp a title on patterned paper and outline and detail with a black journaling pen for an interesting effect. Mount on cardstock, wrap with ribbon and accent with brads for texture.

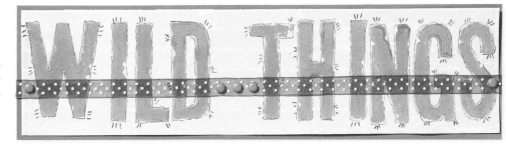

TEMPLATE TITLE

Trace a title onto cardstock with a black journaling pen and then add a subtle spash of color by applying chalk to the upper sections of each letter.

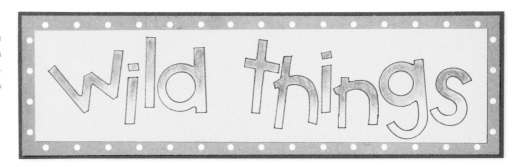

ODDS-AND-ENDS TITLE

Design a wild "ransom-style" title by using letter odds and ends from different letter-sticker and letter-accent sets.

PATTERNED-PAPER TITLE

Put your paper scraps to use by sending them through a die-cut machine for a fun and funky title. Add dimension by inking the letter edges before mounting on cardstock. Staple ribbon scraps along edges for a finishing touch.

Adding journaling

Journaling is a major page accent, and should be considered when adding the title and photos. Strive to write the journaling prior to designing a scrapbook page; it will ensure your desired design can accommodate its length (or, on the contrary, your design won't suffer a gaping hole because you had a case of writer's block). Be sure journaling is legible and accessible on your scrapbook page.

TELLING THE PHOTOS' STORY

Whether printed on paper, handwritten or printed on transparency (as shown here), journaling is a very important part of the layout. It, too, should be part of your overall design. The journaling being added to this page is neat and legible. Before you print journaling or after you have written it, check for misspellings and grammatical errors. If you are including handwritten journaling, warm up by practicing your penmanship before you commit the journaling to your scrapbook page. Also, if you create a separate journaling block that can be attached to your scrapbook page, a mistake means throwing away a small piece of paper, not an entire layout. There are several types of adhesive available to adhere a transparency, including glue dots, adhesive-application machines and spray adhesives. There are also non-adhesive methods to affix journaling, including brads, staples, eyelets or clips.

Adding page accents

Accents are the crowning jewels of a layout, the finishing touch. Experiment with their placement before committing to permanent adhesive. Also, remember that they are called "accents" for a reason. A deliberate sprinkling of accents is usually all you need to finish your masterpiece.

COMPLETING THE PAGE'S DESIGN

These little "coaster" page accents were placed in a visual triangle on the page to help create balance and rhythm. Large accents work great to balance photos and other larger page elements. You can achieve a similar effect by using a group of smaller page elements to balance larger items. In regard to rhythm, identical page accents can repeat each other or mimic shapes, textures and colors found elsewhere in the design. Adhere decorative page accents using appropriate adhesive. Dry adhesives such as foam spacers, photo splits and tape runners work well for paper accents. Wet adhesives like liquid glue work well for clear elements, metal, fabric and ribbon.

The finished page

Sit back. Take a deep breath and exhale. You did it! You're finished and encouraged to soak in the achievement and beauty of your first scrapbook page. See, it's not so hard! With a little thoughtful planning and a few very basic design principles, your memories will go from photos and stories to well-documented works of memory art.

RHYTHM
Floral motifs on the embellishments echo the background paper and create movement across the page.

AN EFFECTIVE TITLE
Sums up the photo and page theme at a glance.

SHAPE AND LINE
Round shapes in the patterned paper play off the angular shapes of the cropped photos. Decorative elements are turned on point to create a third shape. The decorative embellishments also create a visual line for the eye to follow.

A GREAT FOCAL PHOTO
Features a strong focal photo that's been cropped and enlarged for visual appeal.

SYMMETRY
Uses an asymmetric arrangement to create interest.

BALANCE
Dark patterned paper, used in conjunction with the photos, lends equal weight to all parts of the layout.

UNITY
All the photos are matted in the same manner, creating a sense of cohesiveness.

RULE OF THIRDS
Photos and decorative elements are placed strategically at intersecting points to create visual appeal.

SPACE
Bits of white space add breathing room to this busy layout.

GREAT JOURNALING
Helps to tell the story behind the photos.

4

Discovering the Joy of Journaling

If photos are the heart of a scrapbook page, the journaling is the soul. No one denies the power of an endearing and meaningful image. But, if words do not accompany that image, the viewer is left to her own devices to interpret the action, the sentiment, the thought and the reality behind the image.

Countless scrapbookers find journaling to be a challenge. Excuses abound: writer's block or the perceived lack of writing ability, the photo speaks for itself, the journaling is too personal, or there was no room on the page. First, everyone suffers and overcomes writer's block. Second, everyone has the power to express him- or herself through words. Third, photos are inanimate objects—they cannot speak for anyone, let alone themselves. Fourth, there are many ways to conceal journaling if it is too personal to put in plain view. And, finally, there is always room on a page for journaling.

Now that all of the excuses have been put to rest, it's time to see how easy scrapbook journaling can be. This chapter is filled with proven journaling techniques to fill pages with detail and emotion. It also includes ideas for making room for journaling, photo sleuthing and more. Now, time to get that pen and paper ready...you're going to journal!

Who: Haley and her friend Angelina

What: Angelina was spending the weekend with us. The girls decided to do a good deed and rake up the leaves in our neighbors' front yard. They did a great job! I took these photo's when an unsuspecting "Blue" (the cat) came wandering by.

Where: Our neighbors, Gigi and Angela's front yard.

When: Saturday afternoon, Oct. 22nd, '05.

Why: The girls couldn't resist "loving on" the cat a little bit. She's such a sweet cat and what young girl could resist picking her up and giving her some attention? She didn't seem to mind too much.

Why journal?

Journaling is a scrapbook utility—it identifies the people, places and events inside your scrapbook and puts them into a time frame. One of the main reasons people begin to scrapbook is because they are curious about their own ancestors. They only wish their ancestors had kept a photographic and written record of their lives. Be thoughtful to your future progeny—journal on your scrapbook pages so they won't be wondering about you. An added benefit to journaling is the emotional release. Penning your and your loved ones' precious thoughts is unbelievably rewarding.

Scrapbook journaling can be divided into three categories: event documentation, emotive journaling and character study. There are tips relative to each type of journaling that will ease the writing process. Determine what type of journaling your scrapbook page requires and use the following tips to encourage the words to flow.

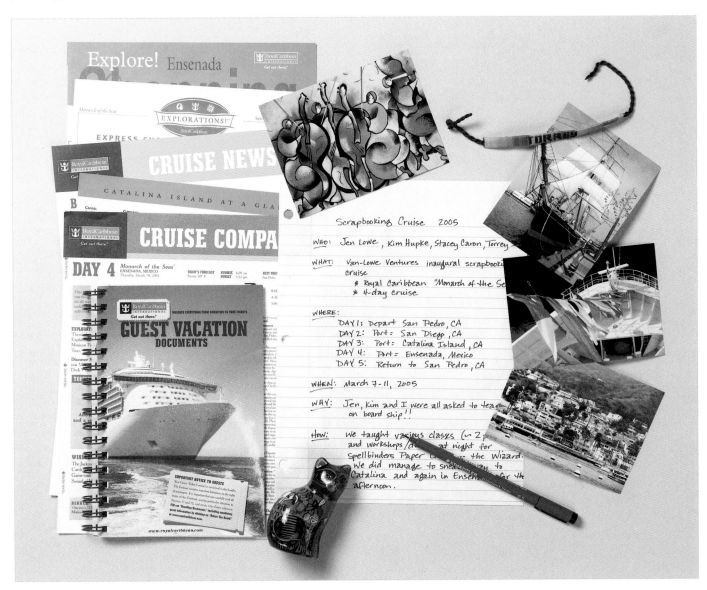

EVENT

When journaling an event, such as a vacation, a holiday, or a wedding, be sure to answer the five Ws and an H (who, what, where, when, why and how). This will ensure that you have all of the facts. If you are having a hard time getting started, pretend you are describing the event to a friend. What is the first thing about the event that you would share? You'll rediscover why this event was important to you and what you want others to know about it. Or, try describing the event using all five of your senses. This will result in lots of detail.

EMOTION

This typically is the most challenging type of journaling. It's personal, and expressing a strong emotion can be difficult. This type of journaling accompanies pages about growth, deep feelings for loved ones, or a hardship. Start by identifying the feeling you wish to convey and look up the definition of that feeling. The definition could help spawn the journaling. Or, try writing the journaling in the form of a letter. Music also can help relax your journaling muscle. Create a mixed CD of songs that either remind you of a loved one or calm you. Listen to it and have a pen and paper handy to jot down inspirations.

CHARACTER STUDY

When you dedicate a scrapbook page to a friend, family member, or yourself, you are creating a character study of sorts. When writing about someone or yourself, start with a word association. What words spring to mind when thinking of this person? Then ask yourself, "Why are these traits so important to who this person is?" Physical descriptions also can unleash ideas. Begin to describe what the person looks like. Think about how you would describe the person to someone who does not know him or her, and include funny or thoughtful anecdotes to illustrate his or her traits.

What to say

If you struggle to find the right words for your journaling, take heart in the fact that, with practice, writing will become more natural. To begin, start with the basics and include them in a short paragraph. Be sure to include people's names, the location of the photo and the date. All it takes is a few sentences to summarize the memory. As you progress as a journaler, challenge yourself to be more descriptive, to include dialogue and to interview family members and friends for their perspectives.

Ineffective journaling

Jessica's original page is lovely to look at but it's missing something vital—journaling. It's difficult, if not impossible, to overstress the importance of journaling in your layouts. Without journaling, future generations will have no clue as to the "who, what, when, where and why" of your layout.

Jessica Sprague, Cary, North Carolina

They say that little boys need men in their lives to teach them how to be men. I have few gifts that compare to the chance to watch the relationship grow between this father and son--this little boy and this man. Jared loves his son with all his heart, and Elliott loves him right back, with the pure delight of babyhood. So far, he saves his biggest grins for his daddy. Who knows if the little one will grow up to be like the big one? I can only watch this team in action, and hope. I can say, though, that nothing would make me happier.

Father & Son

Jared and Elliott

Effective journaling

With substantial, heartfelt journaling added, Jessica's revised layout now looks complete. Her journaling becomes a design element as well as giving her layout richer meaning. Where photos are the body of a layout, journaling is definitely a layout's heart and soul. It not only adds substance and value; it separates a truly meaningful layout from a layout that is simply "eye candy."

Tips for adding personal flair to your journaling

- Include the basic facts: who, what, when, where.

- Show, don't tell. Challenge yourself to use action-packed, detail-laden words that will convey the energy of the photos.

- Include your personal reflections. Photos cannot impart your perception of the event. Use the journaling to describe why the memory is so im-

portant, your favorite part or what you hope to always remember.

- Use poetry, quotes, proverbs or song lyrics to reinforce the page theme.

- Get the opinions of everyone. Ask those who shared in the event for their two cents.

- Pepper journaling with dialogue or anecdotes from the event. Nothing brings a

story to life more than relating a touching moment or a poignant thought.

- Research historical facts. If you are visiting a famous sight, include facts about the location.

- Make it relative. Is history repeating itself? Is the memory an example of a universal human experience? Tell the reader and explain why.

Gathering the facts behind your photos

In scrapbooking, you spend time carefully selecting your favorite photos and designing a beautiful page to house them. Isn't it also worth the time to capture the details behind the photo? If you're working with your own fresh photos, be diligent about jotting notes about the photos once you receive them from the photo finisher. If the photos are from past events and your memory is fuzzy or if they are heritage photos, ask friends and family members if they remember anything. Look in the family Bible in which dates of weddings, births and deaths may be noted. Read old letters, yearbooks and diaries, and ferret out family papers such as wedding and death certificates, mortgage papers, etc. Finally, search the Internet, newspapers and U.S. Census information for clues.

Become a photo detective

If you are lucky enough to inherit heritage photos, you may be unlucky in regard to the lack of information that accompanies them. Identifying and dating unlabeled photos requires a bit of sleuthing. Study the photos for clues.

- Look at the fashions. Pick up a book from the library about fashion through the ages to help.

- Hairstyles, like fashion, also change over time. Research styles or ask a professional stylist for research tips.

- How old are the children in the photos? Kids can be easier to date because of their rapid development changes. Notice their height, weight and the number of teeth they have.

- What kind of car is in the photo? If you can find the make and model of the car, you'll know the photo was taken during or after that year.

- Are any signs, billboards or advertisements visible? Look to them for clues for where and when the photo was taken.

- Study the location of the photo. Does the neighborhood or house look familiar? Was it a family vacation spot? The environment can offer important clues.

KEEPING A PHOTO JOURNAL

Buy a special journal thats only objective is to hold journaling notes about photos. It might be a good idea to buy two—one for organized photos and one for new photos. Label entries so that they correspond to the labels of your photo envelopes. Include details such as the names of those in the images, the date the photos were taken, the location of the events and any thoughts, feelings or layout ideas you have related to the photos.

CONDUCTING AN INTERVIEW

Interview loved ones and friends and use the responses to add life to your journaling. Keep the activity fun and informal. Let the interviewee pick the time and a place where he or she will be most comfortable. It's not a bad idea to send the interviewee a list of questions or topics you plan to cover so he or she can prepare thoughtful answers. Come prepared: Have your list of questions, pens and paper, a tape recorder, and perhaps photos, an old album or yearbook to get the memories flowing. Avoid asking "yes/no" questions. Instead, phrase open-ended questions (those that begin with "what," "why" or "how") that encourage the interviewee to provide explanations and opinions. Be responsive to your subject—nod your head, laugh at funny answers and make eye contact. Keep interview sessions to about an hour and be cognizant of a tiring interviewee.

What your handwriting says about you (and why it should be in your album)

These days, being the recipient of a handwritten message is almost as rare as finding time to take a nap. Everything is e-mailed, typed or conveyed verbally on a voice mail. It's too bad because your personal handwriting is as unique to you as your fingerprint. The way you dot your Is, cross your Ts, curve your Js and connect (or disconnect) the letters of the words you write says so much about your personality. For this reason, you should make an effort to include personal handwriting on your scrapbook pages.

Handwritten page

We all hate our handwriting, but incorporating our own handwriting into our layouts can be as important a part of the layout as the photo itself. Danielle writes her journaling directly on the background paper of her page. It's not perfectly spaced and it kind of runs uphill, but that adds an extremely personal aspect to the page's overall character. So who cares that your handwriting is uneven and imperfect? Your family will love seeing another piece of you on your layouts.

Danielle Thompson, Tucker, Georgia

Including handwriting on a page

Handwritten journaling can be added to any page. Whether it is in plain view or hidden is up to you. Personal handwriting can accompany lengthy computer-generated journaling in the form of short captions comprised of basic information such as names, dates and locations or simple sentiments. Or, it can be added all over the page in a variety of ways.

Writing as a vertical border

Vanessa added vertical journaling directly to her scrapbook page for a personal touch. It's best to practice what you intend to write to lessen the chance of misspellings and errors. Journaling templates exist to help you write in straight lines. Remember, it's not about perfection; it's about leaving an additional touch of personality on your pages.

Vanessa Hudson,
Mount Olive, Alabama

Tips for improving your penmanship

- **Accept your handwriting as is.** Grow to love your handwriting. It may not be perfect (no one's handwriting is), but it is truly your own. These marks are instantly recognizable by your friends and family, and that is something to cherish.

- **Practice, practice, practice.** Musicians rarely take the stage without a warm-up. Warm up your hand by taking a few practice strokes.

- **Find pens and paper you love.** For some, there's nothing finer than a delicate felt-tipped pen when they want to pen loving sentiments. Others prefer a basic ballpoint pen. Find a pen that you like and buy several. It should feel comfortable in your hand and allow you to easily glide across a page. Paper also affects penmanship. Look for acid- and lignin-free paper that gracefully accepts your writing.

- **Keep it hidden.** Some people will never grow to like their handwriting. That is no excuse to exclude it from the ones you love. Simply keep it hidden from plain view by tucking it in an envelope or behind a photo.

- **Mistakes happen.** When you are writing from the heart with the hand, chances are you will write a mistake. Try to prevent mistakes by first relaxing. If you do make a mistake, be creative about covering it up. Use stickers, torn paper strips, correction fluid, etc., and no one will be wise to it.

WRITING IN A SHAPE

Try writing your journaling inside a shape for a personalized page accent. Shape templates can help you corral your journaling while adding to the overall theme and design of your scrapbook page.

WRITING A LETTER

If you don't want to include hand-writing directly on your scrapbook page, consider writing a letter. Be sure to use acid- and lignin-free paper. Ledger patterned paper is available, or you can trace straight lines with the help of a journaling template. If you use a disappearing-ink pen, the lines will vanish, leaving clean, straight script.

WRITING ON A FRAME

Jot sweet sentiments, names, dates, song lyrics and more around a photo frame.

TUCK WRITING IN A POCKET

If you are too shy to put your handwriting in plain view, jot your thoughts, fold them up and keep them safely hidden, yet accessible, inside a pocket.

Making room for journaling

Room for journaling should be considered when you design a scrapbook page. Journaling is the easiest element to provide room for because it can go almost anywhere. Stick it on the page in plain view, or create interactive elements that ask viewers to pull or flip open in order to read it. Personal journaling can be concealed in pockets and envelopes, too. Read on for creative ways to include journaling on your pages.

HIDING JOURNALING

Sometimes we have too much journaling to fit in a little space on a layout. And, sometimes a journaling block would detract from the overall page design. Either of these situations is an indication for hidden journaling. Jennifer's journaling is very extensive but lengthy. Deciding that this much journaling would take up too much space on her layout, she hid it under the hinged focal photo.

Fold-out page

Whether you choose a pullout-journaling block, or to hiding it under a page element, hidden journaling is a wonderful way to incorporate that all-important journaling.

Jennifer Bourgeault,
Macomb Township, Michigan

Printing journaling on a vellum overlay

Because of its translucent quality, journaling on a vellum overlay is a great way to make room for journaling on a scrapbook page without eating up the entire page design. Ginger's vellum journaling block coordinates with other vellum elements on her layout to create journaling that doesn't look like an afterthought. When printing on vellum with an inkjet printer, remember to allow it to dry thoroughly before handling it. This may take up to 24 hours.

Ginger McSwain,
Cary, North Carolina

Printing journaling on a page accent

Another journaling space-saver idea is to apply your journaling to a page accent, such as a tag. Torrey did this by printing her journaling on cardstock and adding it to a tag shape, complete with ribbons.

Torrey Scott, Thornton, Colorado

Simple yet creative journaling styles

In scrapbooking, there exists a multitude of ways to include journaling on a page. From single-word descriptive journaling to bullet-pointed lists and from personal letters to styles that mimic classified ads, you are sure to find at least a few journaling styles that work for your scrapbook pages. Flip through the following pages to find ideas that are not only totally doable, they're also fun!

STRIP-STYLE JOURNALING

This type of quick-and-easy journaling can include single words and simple phrases relevant to your photos and page theme. Simply create handwritten, printed, stamped or "stickered" words and phrases on paper, trim into strips and adhere to the page.

Saying it with simplicity

Whether lined up neat and orderly or placed on your page in a haphazard fashion, journaling strips are a fast and playful way to add that all-important journaling to your layout. Angelia prints her journaling onto cardstock, leaving plenty of room in between each line to allow for trimming it into strips when she's finished.

Angelia Wigginton, Belmont, Mississippi

April 2004 - Unusually warm weather gave Carlie her first taste of running through the sprinkler. She decided to really taste it! She got a nose full of water the few tries. I was delighted to catch the drops of water mid-air in the photos.

PARAGRAPH JOURNALING

This simple journaling style, based on using just a paragraph, focuses on one idea. This one idea explained in the paragraph should be long enough to develop the main idea behind the photos and page theme clearly.

Keeping it short and sweet

Dana's brief journaling paragraph has a beginning, a middle and an ending—just the perfect size for making it into a nifty little page accent, yet long enough to tell the story that it needs to. And there's no reason journaling should look like an afterthought; sometimes just a brief and tiny paragraph is all you need.

Dana Swords, Doswell, Virginia

CHARACTER-TRAITS JOURNALING

This is a fun way to capture in words those little nuances that make your photo subject so endearing and special. Use your imagination to display the character traits in a way that will visually enhance your page theme and layout.

Telling it like it is

This type of journaling—revealing things about others—is not one of the first types of journaling that comes to mind, but it is one of the most effective ways to leave a glimpse into someone's character at any given time in life. Renee's handwritten journaling leads the viewer along a playful path that meanders all over her page while providing lovely insight into the world of her 3-year-old son.

Renee Coffey, Auburn, Georgia

I have always been a dog lover— from a very little girl when I got my first dog at the young age of 3. She was a little buff poodle that I instantly took a liking to because she was sitting in a corner all by herself. I had to go give her some "lovins" and she was the one that went home with us. Well, I brought various dogs home throughout my growing up years and many of them stayed for good. The kind of dog I fell absolutely in love with were cocker spaniels! We had two different ones growing up and I always knew that I wanted one when I had my own house. And I knew that I wanted a black and white one that was spotted all over. I had seen a puppy just like this at one time and just knew that was the exact kind I wanted! Little did I know how hard she would be to find! Our first cocker was a tri color but she was mostly black, cute but not the dream I had in my head. I love Moriah to death but was still on the lookout for that black and white cocker I just had to have!

After years of looking, we decided to mate our female cocker and bought a male, white and buff cocker named Bailey. So now I have two cocker spaniels but still not the black and white one I dream of in my dreams! Well, in October of 2003, my dream came true. We had a litter of puppies and unfortunately all of them died but the one little one that just happened to be black and white. She was so tiny and we didn't know if she would make it! But she did and now I have my dream puppy! She is a little stinker but just too cute! It is amazing to have something you have dreamed about having for so many years finally come to be! Gracie is what we call her and she is very close to my heart!

I LOVE THIS PUPPY.

STORYTELLING JOURNALING

Just as it implies, this type of journaling tells the story behind a photo or photos—complete with a beginning, a middle and an ending.

Expanding on the paragraph to tell a whole story

A layout without journaling is just a bunch of photos. But a layout with substantial journaling is a glimpse into another's life. Journaling should be more than just a regurgitation of the name, date and title of an event. Journaling is what gives a layout character and soul. Heather's heartfelt journaling illustrates much more than just what the picture is about. Her journaling gives the reader insight into Heather herself.

Heather Preckel,
Swannanoa, North Carolina

Turn a memory into a story

- **Go beyond the basics.** A good story moves beyond the basic information (who, what, where, when, why and how) to include the history behind the photos and memorabilia. Research the memory as much as you can to gather all of the facts.

- **Write like you speak.** Most stories have a narrator. Consider yourself the narrator of the memory. As you write, pretend you are sitting in a rocking chair, recounting the events to a roomful of eager listeners. Before you write, try telling it aloud into a tape recorder. Then, transcribe it for the scrapbook page.

- **Have a protagonist and an antagonist.** Most stories involve a main character who must overcome all sorts of obstacles to reach a rewarding end. Consider using this common structure for your own story.

- **Include a beginning, middle, and end.** All stories must have a climax, or turning point; otherwise, what is the point? Be sure to give readers all parts of the story—the beginning, middle and ending. How you structure those parts is up to you. Just be sure the structure propels the plot in a logical manner.

- **Set a mood.** How do you want your readers to feel? Warm and fuzzy? Full of suspense? Scared? Determine a tone and write every word with that tone in mind.

- **Show, don't tell.** You want to involve the reader as much as possible, so you have to be as descriptive as possible. Paint a picture with vivid words. Describe the sights, the sounds, the smells, the tastes and how everything feels. Use active verbs to express strong action.

- **Don't leave anything out.** Your story should include all aspects—the good, the bad, and yes, even the ugly.

- **Have a conclusion.** Don't leave your readers hanging, satisfy them by wrapping up the story with a conclusion. It can be the triumph of right over wrong, the reunion of separated lovers, or a lesson learned.

- **Leave enough room.** This type of journaling tends to be a bit on the long side. Write it before you design your page so you can ensure the proper space for it.

FAVORITES JOURNALING

Similar to character-traits journaling, this type of journaling captures a moment in time with respect to what's going on in the photographs that depict your subject's favorite things.

Revealing that which is near and dear

It's important that your journaling have meaning. One easy way to achieve that is by revealing someone's favorites at any given age. Linda uses a spiraling circle as the format of her telling account of her toddler's love affair with a fruity drink.

Linda Harrison, Sarasota, Florida

LETTER-WRITING JOURNALING

Write your journaling in letter style for the ultimate in personal journaling.

Spilling it all out on paper

With the popularity and convenience of e-mail, writing letters has become a lost art; but it doesn't have to be. Written letters, whether casual memos or formal correspondence, are a unique and touching way to add a personal facet to your layout. Marie uses letter-style journaling as a means of expressing her deepest feelings.

Marie Cox,
Springfield, Massachusetts

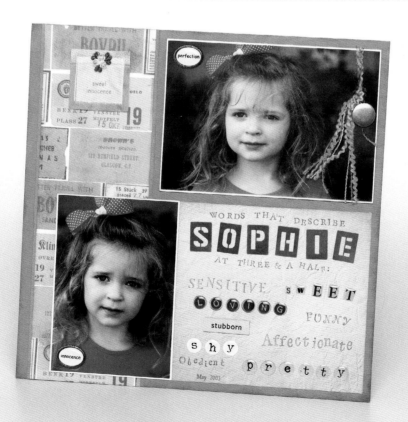

DESCRIPTIVE JOURNALING

This type of journaling uses many adjectives to describe either character traits or what is going on in the photos. The more colorful and creative the adjectives, the more descriptive your journaling.

Highlighting key aspects

There are other methods that add meaningful journaling to your layout besides journaling in prose. Suzy chooses to highlight key aspects of her layout's subject by using a hodge-podge list of descriptive words as her journaling. This type of descriptive journaling employs the use of individual adjectives that describe the subject of the layout to a "T."

Suzy Plantamura,
Laguna Niguel, California

"Do you want to learn to skate?" I asked you one beautiful October day.

The look on your face said, "Are you kidding?"

"I play hockey!" you beamed. "I go get my stick!" And off you went to grab a plastic golf club.

You didn't make it very far on those skates, but between your gear and your t-shirt, you were just too cute. You pretended to be just like the hockey players we had seen at a game just a couple of weeks before. I couldn't resist taking these pictures of my fierce skater boy!

HIDDEN-MESSAGE JOURNALING

Include a secret message within your journaling. It takes a bit more planning and creativity, but it makes for a very special and unique communication.

Concealing a sentiment

You don't have to be a spy to decipher this cute "secret message" style of journaling. Susan creates a message within her journaling by typing key words in a contrasting color. When the highlighted words are read sequentially, they form a secondary sentiment that's too good to be missed.

Susan Cyrus,
Broken Arrow, Oklahoma

CONVERSATIONAL JOURNALING

Think "chit chat" here. Write your journaling as if the photo subject were sitting right there with you.

Documenting a dialogue

Becky preserves an unforgettable bonding moment between her and her daughter through the use of conversational-style journaling. This type of journaling is an excellent way to capture and re-create, word for word, a conversation or discussion that you want to preserve for generations to come.

Becky Thompson, Fruitland, Idaho

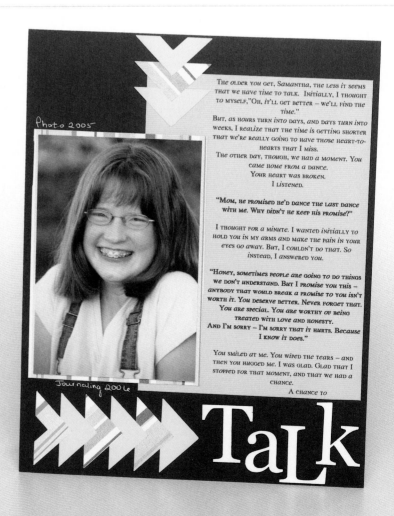

ACROSTIC JOURNALING

Expand on each letter of a word in your page title to express anything from character traits to sweet sentiments about your photo subjects.

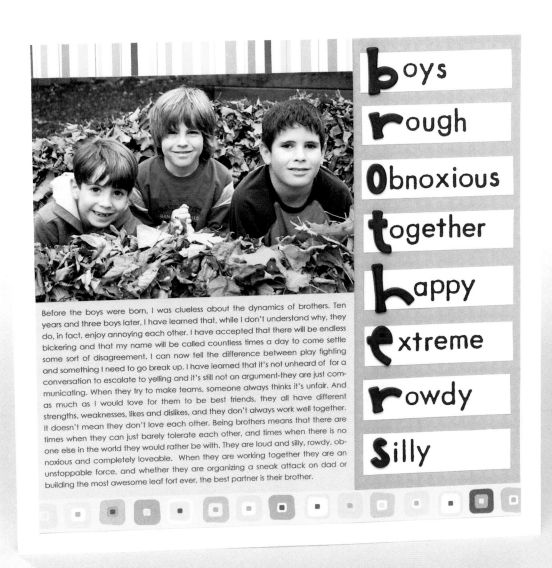

Amplifying a page title

You aren't limited to printed words in a rectangle shape when it comes to journaling. Nicole uses acrostic journaling to create a fun decorative border for her layout. Acrostic journaling is where you take each letter of a word to create descriptors of that word that start with each of the letters.

Nicole Cholet, Beaconsfield, Quebec, Canada

5

Creating Your First Scrapbook Album

Imagine the glee on your child's face as she opens a scrapbook, created by you, points to her photo and squeals, "That's me!" Good luck with trying to hold back the tears. Don't even try to stop the tears welling in your mother's and grandmother's eyes as they sigh and fawn over a newly minted heritage album full of your family's roots and stories. When you become a scrapbooker, you become the family historian, a job with a rewarding responsibility.

Keep this reward in mind when you begin working on your first scrapbook album. Halt creeping intimidation with this sense of duty. Also, the road to a finished scrapbook is paved one page at a time. Set a course of action, and with a little planning, your album will come to fruition quicker, easier and even more painlessly than you think.

Begin with a theme. Then select your photos. Gather your tools and supplies, and get started on your course. What follows is a navigational tool to help you plan your journey. You'll first learn the difference between building a chronological album and theme album. Then, you'll find shortcuts to creating album continuity and how to streamline page construction as well as tricks for including memorabilia.

Chronological albums

Imagine a timeline of your life. A chronological album captures the details of life along this timeline. Chronological albums are a great way to ease yourself into scrapbooking. They follow a simple, logical progression of events. Chronological albums also can be themed. For example, you could create a chronological album of your family life (the theme) by beginning with how you and your husband met, progressing forward to include the birth of children, family vacations and milestones.

Baby album

Kelly's baby album records key moments in her baby's first year of life, month by precious month—starting with a photo of the newborn on the album's embellished cover.

She combines splashes of baby blue with rich reds, pinks and browns throughout her pages to create a unique color palette that unifies her album.

By turning all her photos black-and-white, she adds a feeling of sophistication and formality to this loving tribute to her infant son.

Kelly Goree, Shelbyville, Kentucky

carson and mama

sweet **XO** *kisses*

three months

It's already three months since you were born and I'm even more in love with you today than I was then. So while I'm here and in the moment, I want to take the time to write down a few things I always want to remember about the three month old YOU.

Years from now, I want to remember what it's like to get your sweet baby kisses ever time I would pucker up close to your face...and how ticklish you are and what your tiny, baby giggle sounds like.

I want to never forget the way your face lights up when I walk into a room and that you save your biggest smiles for me. The way you love to be loved and cuddled and squeezed, please. I can't forget that or that sweet baby smell of you.

And in case it changes in the years to come, I never want to forget that you are my only child that ever had strawberry blonde hair and big blue eyes. And Carson, I never want to forget how special I felt when I held you in my arms. I love you, my sweet baby.

XOXO
XOXO

Me album

It's important to include ourselves in our scrapbooks. Susan aptly gives her album cover a simple monogram title.

Susan chronicles her life through pictures that start in her infancy and end with now. Each page is dedicated to a different age with journaling that describes milestones and important events for each age.

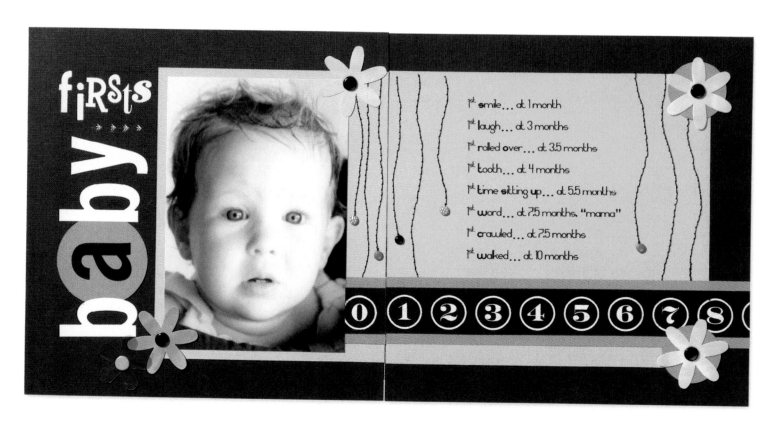

firsts
baby

1st smile... at 1 month

1st laugh... at 3 months

1st rolled over... at 3.5 months

1st tooth... at 4 months

1st time sitting up... at 5.5 months

1st word... at 7.5 months. "mama"

1st crawled... at 7.5 months

1st walked... at 10 months

m e

right now • right here • living life

28 years old • letting creativity be my guide • believing in the power of possibility

:RIGHT

She chooses a pink and black color scheme and floral accents in a graphic design style to reflect her own sophisticated and feminine personality.

Susan Weinroth,
Centerville, Minnesota

loving who i am

and realizing my dreams

NOW

Theme albums

Theme albums are organized by a single subject, which means they usually revolve around an event, a person, a concept (such as an ABC album) or a topic (such as friendship). Theme albums make wonderful gifts, and with the wide selection of mini albums available, projects can be created in a matter of days. Theme albums do require careful planning and a strong sense of unity. A successful theme album will show continuity in regard to paper colors, patterns, journaling and page accents.

Pet album

To start her canine tribute, Kelli chooses an album that comes already decorated with a paw print background. She creates a customized title for her album by adding her own decorative embellishments to the album cover.

Kelli showcases the subject of her album (her dog Riley) with photo-centric double-page spreads that have an enlarged photo on one page with journaling on the opposite page of each spread.

silly

loveable

It is all about the nose. Riley uses his nose to hunt down fallen morsels of food on the floor. He'll use his nose to open the lever-handle on the patio door. And he'll use his nose to nudge his people and garner a pat on the head. Riley even "knocks" on a shut door by rattling it with his nose. Riley got himself (and me!!) into big trouble one day when he used his nose to sniff out the pizza lunch at the elementary school across the street from us. He made a break at the first opportunity and headed to the school to investigate the smell. The boys at the school calmly picked up their lunch trays and watched in amusement as Riley tore through the crowd of children. There were a few girls though, who left their lunch trays on the ground and ran to hug the legs of the playground helpers. Riley gobbled up the abandoned pizza and was quite the happy dog. We still have to keep a close eye on Riley when the school is serving pizza! Yes, Riley's nose knows, and sometimes he puts it where it doesn't belong.

rascal

tHe nose Knows

ROUGH & RUGGED · ROUGH & RUGGED · **R**

CHASING BALLS

Wanna know the truth behind how this picture was taken? The boys and I strung a piece of fishing line through a tennis ball using a needle and then dangled the ball from the deck. I took pictures of Riley as he jumped and tried to get at the ball. Dangling a tennis ball for a 85-pound dog to jump at is a bit of an art. If the ball was too high, Riley wouldn't even make the attempt, but if it were too low, he'd break the ball free from the fishing line and carry it to the corner of the yard where he'd gnaw happily on it. We finally got this shot—Riley dog is a little blurry, but the picture shows to what heights Riley is willing to go to get at a ball. Riley *loves* tennis balls. Loves them more than anything other than food. We take Riley on long walks and he chases either the tennis ball or the floppy disc until he is too tired to run anymore. We have to hide the tennis balls until we are ready to play with Riley or he will go *nuts* begging us to give the ball a toss.

Kelli also creates overall rhythm and unity throughout her pet album by the repetitive use of great imagery, consistent colors and paper choices.

Kelli Noto, Centennial, Colorado

Wedding album

Themed albums lend themselves especially well to a single event—such as a wedding, for example. What better way to start the album than by embellishing it with sweet sentiments.

Lisa captures snapshots of her special day in her beautifully appointed album and generates a completed sense of unity through repeated use of patterned papers, ribbons and other embellishments.

Signing the Marriage License.

Making it legal

Living in LA, we had a lot of legwork to prepare for a NY wedding.

No complaints about our May trip to NYC to apply for the license!

Always fun to visit the City. A Justice of the Peace officiated.

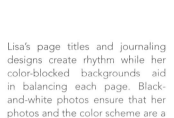

Lisa's page titles and journaling designs create rhythm while her color-blocked backgrounds aid in balancing each page. Black-and-white photos ensure that her photos and the color scheme are a perfect match.

Lisa VanderVeen,
Mendham, New Jersey

Celebration. Cocktails. Music.

Sealed with a Kiss. I love you.

i love you

It was a beautiful summer day. We kept it casual, with a cocktail hour after the ceremony. Such a blissful day. Absolutely perfect.

i love you   i love you   i love you   i love you   i love you   i love you   i love you

Christmas album

Creating theme albums is a great way to get caught up fast in scrapbooking. By organizing two decades of holiday photos and memorabilia by year—and making page kits from every Christmas-related paper and page accent she owned—MaryJo was able to complete a Christmas theme album of wonderful holiday memories in just four weekends.

MaryJo Regier,
Memory Makers Books

Theme-album topic ideas

Theme-album ideas are infinite. Here is a list of ideas, but don't be afraid to search the recesses of your imagination for your own clever themes.

• ABC	• Characters	• Graduation	• Party	• Spring
• Advice	• Children	• Halloween	• Patriotism	• Storybook
• Amusement park/carnival	• Christmases past	• Heritage	• Picnic/BBQ	• Summer
• Animals or pets	• Club/organization	• Hobby	• Pool	• Teen
• Autumn	• College	• Holidays	• Recipes	• Thanks/appreciation
• Baby	• Daily life	• Home/hometown	• Religion	• Thanksgiving
• Baking	• Disney	• Inspiration	• Retirement	• Traditions
• Beach	• Dreams	• Love	• School	• Travel
• Birthday	• Easter	• Memorial	• Scouting	• Tribute
• Calendar	• Family	• Memories	• Seasons	• Wedding
• Camping/fishing	• Fantasy	• Mother's Day	• Shower	• Winter
• Career	• Father's Day	• Moving	• Sisters	• Zoo
• Celebrations	• Floral/gardening	• Nature/outdoors	• Snow	
• Chanukah	• Friendship	• Neighborhood	• Sports	

The album-making process

Every good scrapbook album begins with a solid plan of action. If you take logical steps and don't rush yourself, a completed scrapbook album will be a pure joy to create.

SELECTING A THEME

The first thing you'll want to do is decide what type of album you are going to create. Select a theme and then decide how to organize the album within that theme. Choosing to follow a chronological path is a matter of preference. To select a theme, determine the audience and ask yourself, is this a gift or a family album? Gift albums tend to be smaller than family albums. Will it encompass one event or an event that happens repeatedly each year, such as a holiday? These questions will help you determine the scope of your project.

ORGANIZING PHOTOS/ MEMORABILIA

Head to your stash of organized photos and memorabilia. Select the sets of photos and the accompanying memorabilia that pertain to your album. Spread them out and pick your favorites. Now, group like photos and memorabilia together and arrange those groups in a logical order. This will help you determine page themes and the number of pages your album will require. This is also a good time to select focal photos that may require cropping and enlargements.

SKETCHING DESIGNS

Armed with paper, a ruler and a pencil, you are ready to begin designing your pages (see pages 62-67 for design hints). Sketching your designs will ensure all of your desired page elements will fit neatly onto a layout. It also will help you determine what type and how large of an album you'll need.

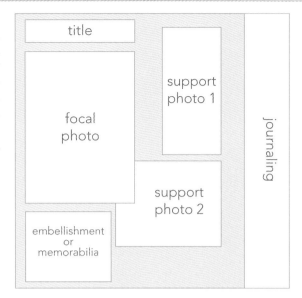

CHOOSING AN ALBUM

When you go to purchase an album, be sure to take your photos and layout sketches with you. Also, purchase any refill pages and page protectors necessary to complete the project. When selecting the album, consider the size and shape of the items you will be displaying. Consider purchasing extra pages so that you can spread out your layouts if you find your photos look too crowded.

PUTTING IT ALL TOGETHER

After you have designed your layouts and purchased your album and supplies, it's time to put it all together. Figure out a process that works for you. Some scrapbookers prefer to create one page at a time, while others treat an album like an assembly line (mount all photos, add all titles, etc.). No matter what method you choose, having all of your photos, memorabilia, tools and supplies organized and at your fingertips will help streamline the process tremendously.

Creating album continuity

Think back to "Designing Your First Scrapbook Page" (pages 54-75). That chapter taught the overarching philosophy behind a well-designed scrapbook page: A well-designed page is balanced, it guides the eye, and most important, it is unified. Consistent use of paper and page accents not only tie together a scrapbook layout, they are the keystones of a unified scrapbook album. Borders can act as bookends, visually embracing sections of your scrapbook. The same title and cropping treatments further add to the cohesion. The tone of the photos and journaling also speak to unify the album.

Ensuring unity throughout a theme album

Theme albums are a fabulous way to showcase a group of photos that are unified by a single theme or event. Start by choosing the topic of your album and gather up all the photos to be used. In this family-centered album, Greta decides to showcase the traits (both physical and otherwise) that members of her family share.

To further unify the pages of her album, Greta repeats the same color scheme and overall design on each and every page. The background paper and physical layout of the background of her page is virtually identical. She constructs titles for each page using the same letter stickers. The final result is a unified and beautiful tribute to the family she loves.

Greta Hammond, Goshen, Indiana

Achieve album continuity design using a variety of patterned papers

Barb records the activities, sights and sounds of a treasured vacation in her travel theme album. Her opening page sets not only the theme but also the tone, colors and design of further pages to come.

Although page 2 of Barb's album uses different patterned papers and colors, she continues the sense of unity established by the first page by using a variety of patterned papers within the same manufacturer's line. She also mixes things up a bit, while still maintaining her overall design, by using the exact layout design in a reversed or "mirror" image.

Page 3 of Barb's album may look familiar; it's supposed to. She uses the exact same layout as her opening page. But, again, she uses a different patterned paper and accent colors for the photo mats and background elements. By simply making very subtle changes like this, her layouts remain interconnected while being just different enough to keep her album interesting from start to finish.

Barb Hogan, Cincinnati, Ohio

Carry continuity through album with imagery and journaling

Suzy captures the spirit of the season in her beautiful holiday-themed album through the use of Victorian images sprinkled on every page. She chooses a single line of coordinating patterned papers to set the mood of her album. The combination of vintage images and color come together to create a sense of warmth and nostalgia—central to her overall theme.

Suzy's direct-to-photo journaling adds a charming personal touch to her scrapbook pages and provides yet another element that unifies her album. Coordinating sticker titles on each page tie everything together in a lovely and unique package.

Suzy Plantamura,
Laguna Niguel, California

Including memorabilia in albums

Memorabilia will add vivid detail to your scrapbook pages. Memories come alive through newspaper clippings, ticket stubs, brochures, historical documents and certificates, maps, postcards, letters, invitations, coins, pressed flowers, locks of hair and any other keepsake that holds the details to a life well-lived. But these keepsakes rarely are of archival quality, which poses a threat to the longevity of your scrapbook pages. This threat can be eliminated with a little planning and ingenuity.

MEMORABILIA SHAPES AND SIZE

Memorabilia come in all shapes and sizes, and those shapes and sizes will dictate how to handle the individual pieces. Paper mementos such as ticket stubs, brochures and postcards can be included on pages inside envelopes and pockets, which also keep them accessible. Consider the weight of the items—thicker or heavier items will need stronger envelopes and pockets. Coins, locks of hair, pressed flowers and other bulky or delicate items should be encapsulated. See the next page for more information. Items that are just too big to include, such as a trophy or school projects, should be photographed for placement on the page.

Tips for preserving memorabilia

Including memorabilia on a scrapbook page can be a challenge, but these tips will help you overcome that challenge.

- Photocopy old documents, certificates and newspaper clippings onto acid- and lignin-free paper. Use the photocopies in your album. Store additional memorabilia in an archival-quality memorabilia box.

- Encapsulate de-acidified or fragile memorabilia.

- Never allow memorabilia and photos to touch.

- When placing photos and memorabilia in close proximity, create barriers between the two. Paper mats help keep acids in memorabilia from migrating to photos.

- Photograph bulky memorabilia, such as trophies or corsages, and include the photos in your album.

- Place memorabilia in archival-quality envelopes and attach the envelopes directly to your page.

- Mount memorabilia with nonpermanent techniques, such as self-adhesive photo corners, so that you can easily remove the pieces to view or color photocopy later.

- When handling old documents, wear cotton gloves to prevent damage from skin oils and dirt.

Encapsulating memorabilia

Encapsulation—putting memorabilia inside photo-safe plastic pockets—makes possible the happy and safe union of photos and memorabilia. Encapsulation systems come in a variety of sizes and include transparent plastic sleeves, keepers and pockets. Any product you choose for encapsulation should be PVC-free and made from polyethylene or polypropylene.

Tips for encapsulating memorabilia

Plastic enclosures, found at scrapbook and hobby stores, offer a wonderful way to feature 3-D memorabilia on scrapbook pages. Use them for coins, keys, pressed flowers, leaves, sand and tiny shells. Pockets or envelopes are great for hair, fur, feathers or other similar items. Sleeves can be used for paper memorabilia, such as birth certificates, postcards or recipe cards. If you are working with maps and other bulky pieces of paper memorabilia, opt for sleeves or pockets.

Prevent memorabilia from scratching photos

Do you have memorabilia you want to include on your layout that's not flat? No problem. There are many containers available that are just made to house even the most lumpy mementos. Melodee adds the perfect keepsake of a favorite outing to her layout—sand. To do this she cleverly adds just a tad to tiny glass bottles and then attaches them to her layout.

Melodee Langworthy,
Rockford, Michigan

Making memorabilia pocket pages

Page pockets will make your scrapbook pages interactive. The pouches beg viewers to reach inside, pull out the contents and fall deeply into the memory contained on the scrapbook page. Pockets can be as simple as a block of paper secured to a page background with adhesive or as elaborate as a folded fabric envelope. See below for pocket ideas and wise tips for adhering them to pages.

Pocket page for flat memorabilia

Want to include memorabilia on your layout? Pockets are a great way to house all those special memories. Becky saves and displays the cards from her daughter's birthday party by placing them in a pocket directly on her layout. Pockets can be customized to any size, shape or color.

Becky Heisler, Waupaca, Wisconsin

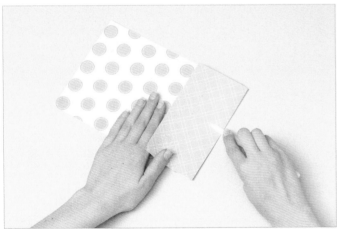

FOLDING MEMORABILIA POCKET EDGES

Making your own memorabilia pockets is easy. To begin, simply create pocket, fold up lower one-fourth of long piece of double-sided patterned paper and crease well with bone folder or fingernail.

SECURING MEMORABILIA POCKET

To secure sides of pocket, staple right and left sides of pocket in three or four places along each edge, leaving upper edge free for the insertion of memorabilia. Instead of a stapler, you can also use an adhesive tape runner to seal pocket edges if desired.

Using page kits to save time

A page kit's ultimate goal is to save you time. Whether homemade or store-bought (see page 53), a page kit includes everything you need to create a well-designed, cohesive scrapbook page or series of scrapbook pages. Both homemade and purchased page kits will save you time shopping and scrapbooking.

HOMEMADE PAGE KITS

If you prefer to create your own page kits, you can do so from your existing stock of supplies. Once you select your photos and memorabilia, gather coordinating paper and embellishments to complement the photos. Complete layout sketches and then organize all of the photos, memorabilia, supplies and sketches into a page protector or page keeper. When you go to a crop (explained in detail on pages 122-123), creating and taking a couple of page kits will help you make the most of your cropping time by allowing you to effortlessly complete pages while you connect with your scrapbooking friends.

6

Connecting in the Scrapbook World

Scrapbooking will provide stronger connections between you, your family and generations to come. It will also connect you to others who share your passion. Scrapbooking isn't simply a hobby, it's a community that will welcome you with open arms.

When starting this hobby, finding friends to share the hobby with will make it less intimidating. Your scrapbooking friends will encourage you to commit to the hobby. They will challenge you to become a better artist. Most important, they will do what any good friend will do—they will listen to you and give you support when you need it.

The best way to enter the scrapbooking world is with friends. These can be friends who already scrapbook and invite you along to a crop, or they can be friends you meet when you take your first scrapbooking class at a local scrapbook store. They can also be virtual buddies that you connect with via the Internet, as it is teeming with scrapbooking message boards and groups.

In these final pages, you will be personally escorted into the scrapbooking community. Read and find out what to expect from classes, discover the Internet resources that are available at your fingertips as well as those that may be offered at your local craft and scrapbook stores. After finishing this chapter, you might begin to visualize yourself taking a vacation at a scrapbook retreat or dreaming about a future "crop" or gathering of scrapbooking buddies you plan to host.

Classes

Scrapbook classes are an excellent way for a newbie scrapbooker to get her feet wet. Get out the phone book and search the yellow pages to find craft and scrapbooking stores. Give those stores a call to see if they offer classes. Ask what types of classes they offer and if you will need to bring anything. In most cases, you'll simply need a few photos to play around with. Bring along a shopping list of basic supplies (don't forget to set a budget to avoid going a little crazy!) and any questions you might have about page ideas, products and supplies, etc. Most scrapbook stores have a cropping room that you can use, sometimes for a small fee, if you'd feel more comfortable having "expert" support to turn to when creating your first pages.

TYPES OF SCRAPBOOK CLASSES

Class topics run the gamut—from beginner "how-to scrapbook" classes to advanced technique classes. Shop around to find classes that are just right for you and where you are in your scrapbooking ability.

Getting the most out of scrapbooking classes

Here are a few general tips that will help you move to the head of the class fast.

- Get a calendar of classes offered, as well as fees, so you can plan accordingly. Sign up for the store's mailing list to help stay in the know about upcoming classes.

- Find out specific store hours and rules for classes in advance. Many classes prefer no babies or children under 10

in attendance. Most will not allow food or drink at the cropping tables.

- Ask what tools and supplies you need to bring, in addition to some photos, as well as what tools and supplies the store offers its class attendees to use—such as punches, decorative scissors and die-cut machines.

- Arrive a few minutes early so you have time to get a good seat and unpack your supplies so you're ready to learn when class begins.

- Take full advantage of class time by participating and asking questions of the instructor and other students around you.

Scrapbook and craft stores

If you live close enough to craft and scrapbook stores, take advantage of these excellent resources. If your store is a scrapbook store, chances are the staff members are scrapbookers themselves. Don't hesitate to ask them questions about products and supplies or seek out advice from them when trying to design pages. If you are visiting a general crafting store, the selection of scrapbooking supplies could be limited to an aisle or two and the store may or may not have scrapbookers on staff. But, the store employees should be knowledgeable about the products and supplies and may be able to direct you to crop groups, classes or other resources.

INSIDE A SCRAPBOOK STORE

Don't be afraid to ask for help. Customer-service clerks at craft and scrapbook stores are trained to answer your questions, helping you to make informed and valuable purchasing decisions.

Becoming a savvy scrapbooking shopper

Going into a scrapbook retail store or the scrapbooking section of a large hobby store can be overwhelming. The tempting and tantalizing products can also be a strain on the budget; it takes great restraint to keep from impulse buying everything you see because there are so many awesome products available. Try taking this store challenge for your first store visit to acquaint yourself with the product before purchasing anything.

- Leave your checkbook, credit cards and cash at home the first time you go—but do bring a small notebook and a pen for taking notes.

- Spend some quality time cruising the aisles, making notes of tools and supplies that interest you as well as writing down prices.

- Read product packaging to learn more about specific tools and supplies, what their intended uses are and how to use them.

- Make notes of specific tools and supplies that relate to your own organizational and page-making needs.

- Ask pertinent questions of salespeople about anything you see or like but do not understand.

- Prior to leaving the store, see if there are any "preferred customer" memberships or cards you can sign up for. Also check to see if there are any coupons available at the checkout stand for your next visit. Sign up for the store's mailing list to receive information about upcoming sales promotions and discount coupons.

- At home, review your notes and prioritize any intended purchases from a budget standpoint, then make a "wish list" so that you are ready for your next store visit.

Libraries and bookstores

Where does a scrapbooker go when she wants to be challenged with new techniques, needs more information than her local scrapbook or hobby store can provide, or is simply curious and wants to know more about this hobby? To the library or bookstore. Libraries and bookstores can each be a clearinghouse of information. Both should have departments dedicated to crafts and hobbies. While the selection of new technique books most likely will be better at a bookstore, the library is a great place to try out books without making a monetary commitment.

SCRAPBOOKING BOOKS AND MAGAZINES

Once you feel comfortable with scrapbooking basics, seek out new knowledge. Books filled with exciting page ideas, new techniques and even the unknown can be found at the local library and bookstore.

Finding scrapbook-related titles at libraries and bookstores

Use these tips for making the most of library and bookstore visits to learn more about scrapbooking.

- Take a notebook and pen with you for jotting down book and magazine titles that interest you.

- Take your library card and the bookstore's frequent buyer discount card, if you have one.

- Consult local libraries and bookstores or click Amazon.com's book search for scrapbooking-related titles.

- Stop at the reference desk or customer-service desk to find out where the craft and scrapbooking-related titles are located.

- Flip through magazines in the magazine section of the library and the newsstand section of bookstores. Familiarize yourself with the various publications available and find one or two that present information in a manner that will be most useful to you.

- Consider subscribing to a magazine or two to help immerse yourself in the world of scrapbooking.

- Visit the library's used-book sale section if available. You never know what treasures you'll find there!

Consumer conventions and retreats

A word of advice in regard to conventions: Set a budget! Scrapbook conventions can be a scrapbooker's dream and a husband's nightmare. Think about it: 10,000 + feet of space dedicated to shopping and classes. Conventions will offer the latest and trendiest products as well as classes from industry experts and celebrities, all eager to share their secrets, tips and favorite products. They are also wonderful places to connect with other scrapbookers and scrapbook manufacturers.

PLAN AHEAD

There are two types of consumer scrapbooking getaways: conventions and retreats. To the right is a benefits breakdown for both, but the following applies to both. Scrapbook conventions are full of scrapbooking super fun, but they can be overwhelming. If you are heading to a convention that focuses on shopping, make a prioritized list of what you would like to purchase. Do a quick online search of those products to check prices. When you get to the show, walk the show floor once before purchasing anything. Make notes of booth numbers and products you like, including prices. Then, evaluate that list before dropping some cash. Check the show's Web site to identify and register for any classes you might be interested in taking. Basically, learn as much about the event as early as possible so you can plan accordingly.

CONVENTIONS

If you want to shop and take classes, this type of show is for you. There are several throughout the year—including The Great American Scrapbook Show (www.greatamericanscrapbook.com)—and they occur all over the United States, which make them great potential day trips. It's a good idea to walk the entire show floor before you make purchases. Check out a consumer scrapbooking show if you want to:

- shop and take classes.
- mingle with everyday scrapbookers as well as professional designers.
- meet and learn new techniques from scrapbooking celebrities.

RETREATS

When you just need to get away, get some pages made and indulge in a little female bonding, look into booking a scrapbooking retreat. Several types exist—decide what type of location you want to spend time at (spa, bed and breakfast, etc.) and begin your hunt. Also, if traveling with friends, be sure to ask about group rates. Always inquire about cropping amenities. Scrapbooking getaways are perfect for those who want to:

- crop, crop, crop.
- enjoy limited shopping.
- have fun with friends and meet new ones.
- get away for a few days.

Preparing to attend a convention or retreat

Scrapbooking retreats and conventions are great places to shop, crop and meet new people. Here are some things to remember to help make the experience more enjoyable.

- Register for shows or classes early and be quick to find a hotel close to the show grounds.
- Wear comfortable shoes.
- Bring a water bottle and light snacks.
- Take an empty, comfortable tote to carry purchases, samples and make-and-take projects (it's a good idea to bring a sturdy folder to protect paper items).
- Have cash handy—it speeds transactions, keeps you on a budget and some food vendors only accept cash.
- Take an address book to keep track of all of the new friends you will meet.

Crops

When more than one scrapbooker gets together to create layouts, the gathering is termed a "crop." Crops can be small or incredibly large. They can be conducted in someone's home, a local craft or scrapbook store, the basement of a church, the local VFW, a convention center or just about anywhere. The main benefits of a crop include are the social aspect as well as the creative synergy that happens in groups. You get to meet and craft with birds of a similar feather. You meet new friends, share supplies, find inspiration and become a better scrapbooker.

Cropping group page

Crops are to scrapbookers what the quilting bee was to our pioneering foremothers. For many, crops are the perfect venue to share not only a common passion but also for camaraderie and to enjoy a little well deserved "me" time. Suzy's bright and cheery layout captures the essence of her scrapbooking club's annual celebration of every scrapbooker's favorite holiday—National Scrapbook Day. The group meets in her garage—a converted wall-to-wall "scrap club." The crops are free and always full.

Suzy West, Fremont, California

Finding a crop group

If you'd prefer to find an established group of croppers to scrapbook with, here are a few tips to help you locate the group for you.

- **Search online message boards.** Visit message boards on Web sites such as memorymakers magazine.com, scrapjazz.com and twopeasinabucket.com to find established crop groups.

- **Visit your local scrapbook store** (LSS). Most LSS's have a bulletin board where customers can post information regarding personal crops. They also serve as scrapbooking community centers—start cropping there and you're sure to find other scrapbookers to crop with.

- **Look in the church bulletin or ask at the local VFW and library.** Many churches, libraries, VFW halls and other community centers will allow crop groups to use their facilities as cropping halls.

Getting organized for a crop

When it comes to cropping-on-the-go, efficiency is key. You want to create a balance between having everything you need and not taking everything you have. With a little planning, you will achieve the perfect balance. If you crop on the go, you will need a trusty bag to handle all of your supplies. Several different types of portable cropping solutions exist. Take stock of what you have before you invest. Also, look at bags and storage containers that were not created specifically for scrapbooking enthusiasts. Tackle boxes, artist totes, even your husband's old toolbox could be just the right storage solution for you. There are some supplies that you will need every time you scrapbook.

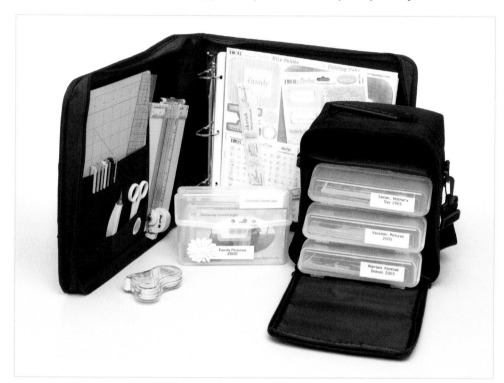

Cropping on-the-go

Use the following list to help you get organized for a crop. This list covers the basics; as you attend more crops, tailor it to suit your personal needs.

- Adhesives
- Basic shape template
- Black journaling pens
- Blank scrapbook pages
- Colored pencils, pens and markers
- Corner rounder punch
- Craft knife
- Decorative scissors
- Metal straightedge ruler
- Page kits (see pages 52-53 for more information)
- Page protectors
- Paper trimmer
- Pencil with eraser
- Scissors
- Small assortment of colored cardstock
- Small cutting mat

HOSTING YOUR OWN CROP

Use these tips to be the crop hostess with the mostest:

- Invite the perfect amount of people. Take note of how many croppers you can comfortably accommodate and don't invite more than that. If your group of cropping friends is more than you can handle, simply state that space is limited and RSVPs will be accepted on a first-come basis. This is also a wonderful opportunity to introduce a friend to scrapbooking. If your home will not permit more than a few scrapbookers, seek out an alternate location, such as a church or local library.

- Schedule the crop so that it won't interfere with hectic lives. Is your crop group comprised mostly of working moms? If so, try to avoid scheduling the crop during a

time that will be hectic for your group, such as during dinnertime or on Saturday mornings when soccer moms are required to be gameside.

- Schedule the crop for a set amount of time. Consider this a favor to yourself. If you set a time limit, guest croppers will be less likely to overstay their welcome. Be sure to enforce the end time by politely thanking guests for coming.

- Serve non-greasy, non-messy snacks and plan for 30 to 45 minutes of socializing. Greet your guests with "clean" snacks such as butter-free popcorn or dessert and coffee and allow everyone to chat for a bit before you get down to scrapbooking. Use this time for "show and tell," and encourage members to share recently

finished pages or new ideas with the group.

- Encourage fellow croppers to share more expensive nonconsumable supplies. Don't force anyone to bring anything that is too inconvenient, but politely suggest that group members can bring portable die cutters, adhesive-application machines and other fun "toys."

- Play games and have prizes. Easy, fun games can be arranged and prizes awarded. Hold a contest to see who can create the most pages in one sitting or challenge croppers to try a new and exciting technique. Prizes can be a gift basket of clean but used supplies or a gift certificate in a small amount to the local craft or scrapbook store.

What's available on the Internet

The information superhighway is a scrapbooker's route to just about anything she needs. Perform a Google search for the term "scrapbooking" and more than 6 million Web sites will be found. At your fingertips are Web sites for shopping, connecting with other scrapbookers, viewing layouts, finding information about products and techniques, registering for scrapbooking retreats, organizing swaps, and so much more!

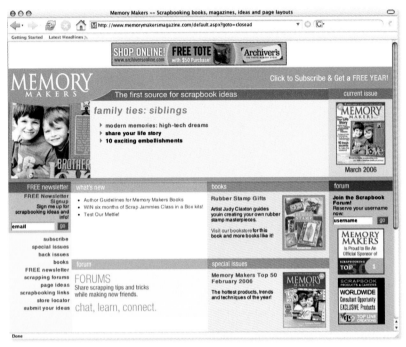

SCRAPBOOKING WEB SITES

Scrapbooking Web sites such as www.memorymakersmagazine.com provide a wealth of information for both beginning and established scrapbookers.

Ten reasons every scrapbooker should be online

Whether you want to shop or simply view other scrapbookers' layouts, the Internet is teeming with resources for today's modern scrapbooker.

1 **Comparison shop.** If you're looking to purchase an expensive supply, such as a crop bag or die-cutting machine, do a little online research to see which brand will give you the most bang for your buck.

2 **Shop.** Perhaps the nearest local scrapbook store is two hours away, or maybe you just don't have time to visit the local store. Shopping for scrapbooking supplies online will give you a great selection of supplies from the comfort of your own home, any time of day.

3 **Meet friends.** Hundreds of Web sites are online depots for scrapbookers to connect with each other. Message boards often have multiple chat categories, allowing users to log on to talk about scrapbooking, getting published, family life and more.

4 **Find resources.** The Internet is called the "information superhighway" for a reason. It contains a wellspring of information on any technique or product you care to know about.

5 **Register for a scrapbooking retreat.** Are you ready to take that scrapbooking vacation you've always dreamed of? Search the Internet for the one that is best for you.

6 **Swap page kits and accents.** Swaps are one of the most popular ways for scrapbookers to connect. See the next page for more details.

7 **Help a good cause.** Use your scrapbooking for the power of good. Search for scrapbooking charities, organize your own crop group for a charitable cause or volunteer for a therapeutic scrapbooking program.

8 **Win stuff.** The Internet is a wonderful place to find contests. Contest challenges range from creating layouts to writing heartfelt journaling. Prizes range from gift baskets to cruises!

9 **Sell your stuff.** If you're looking to unload all of those Disney stickers you bought in a frenzy following the family trip or wish to sell your gently used die-cut machine to help offset the cost of your new one, head to the Internet. Auction sites, such as eBay, have been helping scrapbookers waste-not-want-not.

10 **Get published.** Several online scrapbooking critique groups have formed with the sole purpose of getting members published. Members post layouts to the group and receive constructive criticism regarding the layout design.

Swaps

A swap is the modern-day scrapbooker's bartering system. Organize a swap so you and your cropping buddies can exchange unused supplies, or hold them to exchange homemade page kits, cards or accents. Swaps can be held in your home or organized over the Internet. Some Internet crop groups will organize a swap prior to meeting at a scrapbooking retreat. Once at the retreat, the group members trade their goods.

SWAPPING TOOLS AND SUPPLIES

If you already know some scrapbookers and perhaps already have a small arsenal of tools and supplies yourself, consider hosting a tool and supply swap! Swapping one unwanted item for an item you will use can be a great way to grow your stash of useful tools and supplies.

How to host a swap

Here are a few tips to help you organize your own swap, at home and online.

In-home swaps

- Send out invitations at least two to three weeks in advance. Be sure to include the time, location, RSVP information and what to bring.

- Pick a theme for the swap. Consider swapping bags of patterned paper, page kits, handmade cards or themed items (such as birthday or holiday).

- Arrange items on a large table with lots of open space.

- Make it a party. Play festive music and have clean snacks for your guests to munch on while they swap.

- Provide pens, price tags and tally sheets for guests to keep track of trades or purchases.

Internet swaps

- Determine a swap format. Internet swaps require special logistical concerns. Will all of the participants send a chosen item to the host, who then will distribute them? Will the swap be organized so that it will take place at a later date in a physical location? Will group members connect one-on-one and swap items?

- Pick a theme for the swap. Will you swap page kits, packs of homemade cards or accents or supply goody bags?

- Get information to group members. You can e-mail the specifics or post on an online message board.

- Remind participants to include correct postage on their swap parcels or shipping boxes.

- E-mail participants to confirm the receipt of their packages.

- Regularly post the status of the swap on the appropriate Internet message board.

- Be punctual in sending swapped materials to participants.

- For more information, do an Internet search for "scrapbook swaps."

Critique groups

Once someone has been bitten by the scrapbooking bug, it usually is not long until she craves to be published. Scrapbookers consider it a high honor to be published in a magazine or book and on Internet scrapbooking sites. It validates their artistic creativity, and who doesn't want to show off their precious families to the world? Critique groups allow scrapbookers to receive constructive criticism from their peers.

ORIGINAL LAYOUT

Heidi Finger, Brighton, Colorado

REVISED LAYOUT

ORIGINAL LAYOUT

Heidi is brand-new to scrapbooking. She found a critique group helpful in teaching her to see what could be better about her layout. They agreed her choice of colors was good, but they had some suggestions for improving her layout overall. Although she had a focal point due to photo placement, the group suggested that a more predominant focal photo was needed. They also taught her about the rule of thirds and encouraged her to consider using only three photos on her layout instead of all four They also felt that her title seemed to get lost on the page; it needed to be stronger and carry more weight. The next step was to incorporate other design principles in her layout: rhythm, balance, line and shape. As the finishing touch, they advised her to make her journaling look less like an afterthought.

REVISED LAYOUT

Armed with valuable insight, information and inspiration, Heidi employs all the recommendations made by her critique group. By enlarging and creatively matting her focal photo, it now commands a place of honor on her layout. She chooses three photos and arranges them to form a visual triangle on her page. No longer will her title be denied. It now pops off the page and takes charge for all to see. Circular shapes echo the main patterned paper, creating rhythm. She achieves balance through the weight and placement of all the page elements. By placing her journaling on a transparency, it now blends with her page. Its curved line hugs the profile of the space in which it's placed, making it appear as part of the overall design and not just an afterthought. Her layout went from "so-so" to "so amazing" with a little help from her friends.

Starting your own critique group

Take this advice when starting or joining a critique group.

- **Seek out people of trust.** Your group should consist of a small, tight-knit group of cropping friends you can trust to dispense honest and constructive advice.

- **Do not "scrap lift" or steal ideas for profit from the group.** Group members respect the integrity of everyone's work.

- **Limit the number of participants.** Try to keep the group between 10 and 20 members.

- **Be specific with critiques.** Show, don't tell, members why you like or dislike an aspect of their layout. Also, be generous with praise, too.

Mail-order clubs

Joining a mail-order club is like hiring a personal shopper to buy your scrapbooking supplies. If you are a member of a club, you can expect a box of preselected coordinating product to arrive on your doorstep on a regular basis. More than a hundred active clubs can be found online, and they range in specialty from stamping to paper crafts. Members of mail-order clubs can be found wriggling with anticipation when waiting for a regular shipment of scrapbooking goodies. Club operators try their best to fill their respective goody boxes with only the latest and greatest supplies, not to mention ideas for using the supplies. Clubs also offer a way for the members to connect via message boards.

SUPPLY CLUBS

Club Scrap (www.clubscrap.com) offers members a chance to discover the unexplored areas of their creativity by providing unique and superior materials along with a forum for the exchange of innovative ideas and techniques.

Becoming a club member

Scrapbook clubs shop for their members, saving them time, frustration and energy in the store, struggling to coordinate products. Many clubs also host online communities. Here are a few things to keep in mind before becoming a club member.

- **Know yourself.** Do you like surprises? Some clubs pride themselves on surprising their members each month, while others offer members a choice in supply selection from a short list of options.

- **Know your style.** Do you love cardstock or are most of your pages made with patterned papers? Are you a sticker maven or a rubber-stamp goddess? When choosing a club, sign up for the one that most closely matches your sense of style.

- **Do your homework.** Do some research to help understand the difference between vari-ous clubs. Perform a Google search with the keywords "scrapbook club." Seek out information on clubs that interest you, read their Web site FAQs or call and ask for samples and brochures. Ask friends about their club memberships and ask to see their club kits for yourself.

- **Not every club is for everyone.** Just because your friend loves one club doesn't necessarily mean that you will.

- **Read the fine print.** If you sign up for six months, you'll probably have to get all six months' worth of kits before you can cancel.

BOOK CLUBS

The ScrapBook Club (www.thescrapbookclubonline.com) is the first and only book club exclusively for scrapbookers. Through The ScrapBook Club, you'll receive great discounts on a selection of the newest and best scrapbooking books, plus you'll be part of a community of other scrapbookers who love to share ideas and inspiration.

Glossary of scrapbook terms

3-D PHOTOS
Using foam spacers between layers of photos to add depth and dimension and to create 3-D photo art.

A

ABSTRACT SHAPES
Simplified versions of natural shapes, such as symbols denoting restrooms.

ACHROMATIC COLORS
A colorless scheme comprised of blacks, whites and grays.

ACID-FREE
In chemistry, materials that have a pH of 7.0 are neutral. Although acids were once prevalent in photo album papers and products, the damage caused by acids to photographs and memorabilia has been realized and should be avoided. Look for scrapbook products—particularly papers, adhesives and inks—that are free from destructive acids that can eat away at the emulsion on your photos. Harmful acids can occur in the manufacturing process. Check labels for "acid-free" and "photo-safe."

ADHESIVES
A far departure from the gloppy glues of the past, modern adhesives come in both "wet" and "dry" applications depending on one's needs and are used to adhere photos, accessories and memorabilia to scrapbook pages. Buy and use only acid-free and photo-safe adhesives.

ALBUM

page 28

The archival-quality book in which you place your finished scrapbook pages for posterity and for safekeeping. Available in a number of shapes and sizes, albums secure pages in post-bound, binder, spiral or strap-hinge style. Archival albums should be purchased in place of the previously popular magnetic albums, which can destroy photos and memorabilia.

ANALOGOUS COLORS
Colors located next to each other on the color wheel.

ARCHIVAL-QUALITY
Nontechnical term that suggests a material or product is permanent, durable or chemically stable, and that it can be used safely for preservation purposes.

ASYMMETRY
Method of creating balance in which different objects with equal weight are distributed on a page.

B

BALANCE
Equal distribution of weight on a page to create a pleasing arrangement of elements.

BLEEDING
Method of manipulating space in which elements extend over page edges.

BORDER
The upper, lower and side edges or margins of a scrapbook page. Sometimes refers to a border design that is handmade or manufactured and attached to a page.

BUFFERED/ALKALINE RESERVE
Buffering prevents the formation of acids within paper and protects it from exposure to secondary acids from memorabilia, other paper, glues, the atmosphere and oil from fingertips.

BUFFERED PAPER
Paper in which certain alkaline substances have been added during the manufacturing process to prevent acids from forming in the future due to chemical reactions.

C

CARDSTOCK

page 31

The heaviest of scrapbook papers; can be solid-colored or patterned. While also used for die cuts and pocket pages, many scrapbookers now look to the innumerable colors of cardstock to serve as page backgrounds.

CD-ROM
A compact disc that can store large amounts of digitized photos and data files. In scrapbooking, font and lettering CDs as well as scrapbook software CDs have become helpful tools in individually personalizing the page-making process.

COLLAGE

Collage is a collection of different elements adhered together on a page and usually includes photos, embellishments or craft supplies. The elements may or may not overlap.

COLORANTS

page 46

Colorants include a wide array of pens, markers, ink pads, chalks, paints and pigment powders—each with its own distinct characteristics and unique properties—made specifically for scrapbooking.

COLOR WHEEL

Artist's tool for matching and coordinating colors, arranged in a circular fashion.

COMPLEMENTARY COLORS

Colors located directly across from one another on the color wheel.

CONCEPT

A central idea or overall theme for a scrapbook page.

CONTRAST

Variations and differences between light and dark colors.

CROP

A term utilized by enthusiasts to describe an event attended by scrapbookers for the purpose of scrapbooking, sharing ideas and tools and swapping products; held at conventions, craft and scrapbook stores, private homes, organized craft events and crop-oriented vacations.

CROPPING

The act of cutting or trimming photos to enhance the image, eliminate unnecessary backgrounds or turn the photos into unique works of art. Early albums most typically displayed photos in their entirety; safe and easy cropping tools have effectively undermined the notion that photographs should not be altered by means of cutting.

D

DE-ACIDIFICATION

To chemically treat paper or memorabilia with a solution that neutralizes acids and builds up an alkaline reserve, which helps prevent future acid migration from damaging photos.

DECORATIVE SCISSORS

page 35

While pinking shears were once a fancy departure from traditional straight-edge cutting, there now exists a multitude of scissors with special-cut blades or teeth that provide a wide array of cut patterns, designs and cutting depths. Flipping decorative scissors over will result in a varied cutting pattern.

DIE CUTS

page 28

Precut for purchase or self-cut paper shapes that come in both printed and solid colors. Decorative elements for adding a theme or accent to a page. Should be acid- and lignin-free.

DIGITAL

A computer-related term for the process of using numerical digits to create uniform photographic images as shot with a digital camera or scanned into a computer with a scanner.

DIRECTION

The logical path that your eyes should follow through a design.

DISTRESS

A creative technique, such as sanding, used to "age" photos, papers and page accents.

DOUBLE COMPLEMENTS

Pairs of complementary colors used together.

DURABILITY

An item's ability to resist the effects of wear and tear from use.

E

EMBELLISHMENTS

page 48

Page accents that you make or buy. Includes stickers, die cuts, stamped images and punch art. May also include baubles (beads, buttons, rhinestones, sequins), colorants (pens, chalk, inkpads), metallics (charms, wire, jewelry-making components, eyelets, fasteners), textiles (ribbon, embroidery floss, thread) or organics (raffia, pressed flowers and leaves, tiny shells, sand). While one-dimensional accessories traditionally adorned scrapbook pages, there now exists a limitless array of cutting-edge and even three-dimensional products that may be safely used on scrapbook pages.

EMBOSS

One of several creative techniques—including wet, dry and heat embossing—used to impress an image or raise an image in a relief.

EMPHASIS

The idea of making a certain element of a design stand out.

ENCAPSULATE

page 19

To encase paper or three-dimensional memorabilia in PVC-free plastic sleeves, envelopes and keepers for their own preservation and the protection of your photos.

F

FIBER-BASED PAPER (FB)

A photographic paper used to develop black-and-white photographs. Because of the way it is made, fiber-based paper can have a 200-year life expectancy (if taken care of and processed correctly). Formerly, it was the standard type of photographic paper, but today fiber-based paper is mainly used for fine-art black-and-white prints.

FOCAL POINT

The central place in which one's attention is drawn in a photo or on a layout.

FONT

A font is a complete set of characters in a particular size and style of type. This includes the letter set, the number set and all of the special character and diacritical marks you get by pressing the shift, option or command/control keys.

FRAMES

Cropping frames for photos is an easy way to add class to your photos without taking attention away from the photo's subject.

G

GEOMETRIC SHAPES

Structured shapes such as circle, square, rectangle, triangle, etc.

GRID

The structured, underlying framework of a design.

H

HIERARCHY

A system of organizing information in a design so that the most important elements are emphasized and noticed first.

HUE

The particular shade, lightness or darkness of a color.

I

INITIAL CAP

The first letter of a title or paragraph, designed differently so that it stands out from other elements.

INTENSITY

The strength of a color as related to the purity of that color.

J

JOURNALING

page 86

Handwritten, handmade or computer-generated text that provides pertinent details about what is taking place in the photographs.

K

KEY COLOR
Dominant color in a color scheme.

L

LAYOUT
The final arrangement of paper, title, photos, journaling and page accents on a scrapbook page.

LIGHTFASTNESS
A color which is resistant to the action of external agents, such as light, acids, alkalis.

LIGNIN
An organic substance (sap) which acts as a binder for the cellulose fibers in woods and certain plants. It is undesirable in the production of fine papers as it reacts with light/heat to produce phenol (alcohol) and acids which cause deterioration and embrittlement of paper.

LIGNIN-FREE
Paper products that are void of the material (sap) that holds wood fibers together as a tree grows. Most paper is lignin-free except for newsprint, which yellows and becomes brittle with age.

M

MATTING
The act of attaching paper, generally cropped in the shape of a photo, behind the photo to separate it from the scrapbook page's background paper.

MEMORABILIA

page 19

Mementos and souvenirs saved from travel, school and life's special events—things that are worthy of remembrance.

MONOCHROMATIC COLOR
Various shades, hues, tints or tones of one color.

MOOD
The feeling created by choosing certain elements and colors to form a layout or design.

MOSAICS
Pieced photo mosaics are a captivating way to display photos, whether you are cropping and reassembling a single photo or combining several photos.

MOUNTING

page 71

Process of attaching photos or memorabilia to an album page. Permanent mounting requires the application of adhesive to the back of a photo or mat. Nonpermanent mounting allows you to attach your items to a page and still have the option of easily removing them.

N

NATURAL SHAPES
Figures occurring naturally such as the human body, plant and animal shapes.

NEUTRAL COLORS
Black, white, gray, brown and tan.

NON-BLEEDING
A term that describes an ink that does not spread from the original mark on the paper's surface. Non-bleeding depends on both the degree of sizing in the paper and the use of solvents (other than water) in ink.

NON-PERMANENT MOUNTING
Using photo frames, photo corners or pocket sleeves to hold pictures and memorabilia on a page without permanently adhering them.

O

OPTICAL WEIGHT
The appearance of heaviness or lightness and balance in design, determined by positioning of elements.

ORGANIZATION

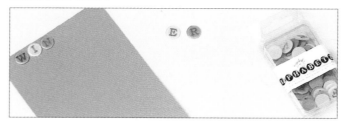

page 49

The act of putting together photos and memorabilia for the purpose of scrapbooking. Organization of scrapbook tools and supplies provides for maximum scrapbooking efficiency.

P

PAGE PROTECTORS

Plastic sleeves or pockets that encase finished scrapbook pages for protection. Use only PVC-free protectors.

PAGE TITLE

page 73

A general or descriptive heading put on a scrapbook page that sums up the theme or essence. Conversely, a "title page" is the first at the front of a scrapbook, often decorated and embellished (without photos), that describes the book's content.

PERMANENCE

Ability of a material to resist chemical deterioration, but not a quantifiable term. Permanent paper usually refers to a durable alkaline paper that is manufactured according to ANSI/NISO standards.

PH

The symbol for the degree of acidity or alkalinity of a substance. A pH value of 7.0 is neutral. Less than 7.0 is acidic, more than 7.0 is alkaline.

PHOTOGRAPHIC ACTIVITY TEST (PAT)

A series of tests designed to identify reactivity of photographic images to various elements.

PHOTOMONTAGE

Montage is similar to collage, but the pictures or parts of pictures are superimposed or overlapped so that they form a blended whole. Photomontages are made strictly of photos, with no other scrapbook embellishments.

PHOTO-SAFE

A term used by companies to indicate that they feel their products are safe to use with photos in a scrapbook album.

PIGMENT INK

Water-insoluble colorants suspended in a liquid—either water, oils or other carriers. Pigments do not penetrate the surface being colored. Instead they adhere to it, providing better contrast and sharpness. For journaling pens and inkpads, look for "acid-free" and "photo-safe" on the label.

POCKET PAGE

page 114

A scrapbook page that includes some form of a "pocket" in which to place memorabilia or journaling.

POLYETHYLENE (PE)

A polyolefin made from propylene gas. Polypropylene, when free of coatings and additives, is chemically stable. (Used in reference to page protectors.)

POLYVINYL CHLORIDE (PVC)

A plastic that should not be used in a scrapbook because it emits gases, which cause damage to photos. Use only PVC-free plastic protectors and memorabilia. Safe plastics include polypropylene, polyethylene and polyester or Mylar.

PRESERVATION

The act of stabilizing an item from deterioration through the use of proper methods and materials that maintain the conditions and longevity of the item.

PRIMARY COLORS

Red, yellow and blue; no other colors can be mixed together to create these colors.

PROPORTION

The comparative relationship between elements of a design with respect to size, amount and degree.

PUNCHES

page 39

Tools in which paper is inserted and pressure is applied to produce particular shapes through a bladed configuration.

R

RECYCLED PAPER

Paper that meets minimum reclaimed-content standards established by federal, state and municipal governments and the paper industry. Fiber content usually consists of post- and pre-consumer reclaimed fiber plus virgin pulp.

REPETITION

Including the same or similar elements more than once in a layout to create rhythm.

REVERSE-IMAGE

Reverse-image photos are useful when a mirrored photo effect is desired.

RHYTHM

Rhythm is a term most commonly associated in scrapbooking with creating visual rhythm within design. Rhythm results from a pattern with both repetition and variation of shape, size, color, line, texture or other details. It creates the illusion of movement or motion, which in turn adds energy and excitement to your scrapbook pages.

RULE OF THIRDS

Concept that divides a space into nine equal sections with vertical and horizontal lines; for a pleasing composition, your subject should fall on or near any of the points where the lines intersect.

S

SANS SERIF

A type style without finishing lines on the ends of letters.

SECONDARY COLORS

Purple, green and orange; colors derived by combining primary colors (red + blue = purple, yellow + blue = green, yellow + red = orange).

SEPIA

A photograph printed in monochromatic brown tints.

SERIF

A type style with tiny lines that finish off the ends of each letter.

SHADE

The degree to which a color is mixed with black.

SHAPE CUTTERS

page 35

Bladed tools that are useful for cropping photos, mats and journaling blocks into perfect shapes. They can cut in circles, ovals and many other simple shapes.

SHAPES

Whether freehand cut or cropped with the use of a template, shape cropping adds simple style to scrapbook theme pages while narrowing the focus of the photo's subject.

SKETCH

A sketch is a hand-drawn or computer-created blueprint or drawing that shows the approximate placement of a title, journaling and photographs on a layout.

SPACE

The distance or area between or around page elements.

STAMPS

A wood, rubber or clear acrylic tool used to impress a design on paper or cloth; used with a stamp pad or inkpad.

STICKERS

page 40

Gummed with adhesive on one side and a design or pattern on the other, stickers are one of the easiest ways to embellish scrapbook pages.

T

TEMPLATES

Templates are stencil-like patterns made of plastic, metal, sturdy paper or cardboard.

TEXT PAPER

A general term for lightweight papers—commonly used for stationery. Text paper is an uncoated printing paper of unusually high quality, available in a wide range of finishes and colors.

TEXTURE

A creative technique, such as crumpling, used to add coarseness or bulk to flat papers.

V

VINYL

See polyvinyl chloride.

Additional instructions & credits

Cover

Albums (Colorbök); decorative scissors, small scissors, craft knife (Fiskars); punch (EK Success); journaling pens (Staedtler); chalk inks (Clearsnap); adhesive runner (Tombow); ribbon (American Crafts); cardstock; buttons; eyelets; ruler; journal; pencils; Photos: Kelli Noto, Centennial, Colorado

Page 1

Photo file boxes (MBI); adhesive runner (We R Memory Keepers); scissors (Fiskars); pens (Staedtler); paper trimmer, corner punch (EK Success); album (Colorbök); ribbon (American Crafts); paper flowers (Prima)

Page 3

Album (Colorbök); embellishments (Chatterbox)

Pages 6-7

Cropping tote with removable scrapbook (Handbags Full of Memories); page manager (Smead); patterned paper, paper accents (My Mind's Eye); scissors (Fiskars); adhesive (EK Success); ribbon; buttons

Pages 8-9

Photo file boxes (MBI); lightbox (Artograph); preservation sprays (EK Success, Krylon, Photographic Solutions); paper flowers (Prima); archival gloves (Highsmith)

Page 10

Photo file boxes (MBI); plastic folders (Generations); pen (EK Success)

Page 17

Negative file sleeves (Print File); negatives box (Light Impressions); preservation spray (Photographic Solutions); archival gloves (Highsmith)

Page 18

Memorabilia storage (Generations, Smead)

Page 19

Page protectors, dividers (Generations); preservation spray (EK Success); memorabilia holders (Deja Views, Fiskars)

Page 21

Photos: Kelli Noto, Centennial, Colorado

Pages 24-25

12" rotary paper trimmer (Tonic Studios); ergonomic craft knife, scissors (Fiskars); Herma Dotto adhesive dispenser, corner rounder punch (EK Success): letter stamps (Hero Arts); glimmer chalk (Craf-T); ribbon (American Crafts); Triplus fineliner pens (Staedtler); brads, buttons, acrylic letters and sayings (Junkitz)

Page 26
Consumables

Adhesive remover (un-du); die cuts (source unknown); cat's eye ink pad (Clearsnap); solvent ink pad (Tsukineko); glue roller (Saunders); pigment pens (American Crafts, Staedtler); patterned paper (Me & My Big Ideas); epoxy stickers (Creative Imaginations); solid paper

Page 26
Non-consumables

Craft knife, cutting mat (Hunt); paper trimmer, scissors (Tonic); corner punch (EK Success); ruler (C-Thru Ruler); shape cutter (Fiskars); letter stamps (Hero Arts)

Page 27
Tools already owned

Adhesive remover (un-du); craft knife, scissors (Fiskars); cutting mat (Marvy/Uchida); combination graphing/metal straightedge ruler (Creative Impressions); removable artist's tape (3M); adhesive runner (We R Memory Keepers); tweezers

Page 27
Other tools

Crimper (source unknown); decorative scissors, paper edger ruler (Fiskars); template (C-Thru Ruler); crystal lacquer (Sakura Hobby Craft); cat's eye pigment ink pad (Clearsnap); blending chalks (Plaid)

Pages 28-29
Albums

Decorative albums (Colorbök); three-ring binder (We R Memory Keepers); spiral (DMD); postbound (C.R. Gibson); strap-style (Westrim)

Page 31
She's Got It!

Supplies: Patterned papers (Scenic Route Paper Co.); ribbon, brads, paper flowers (Making Memories); letter stickers (Memories Complete)

Page 31
Organizing and storing paper

Cardstock (Prism Papers); patterned papers (Me & My Big Ideas); paper organizer (Novelcrafts)

Page 32
Dry adhesives

Adhesive runners (EK Success, Saunders, Tombow); adhesive-application machines (Xyron); photo splits (Therm O Web); photo tape (3L, 3M, Therm O Web); foam adhesive (Ranger, Therm O Web)

Page 33
Wet adhesives

Wet adhesives (Beacon Adhesives, EK Success, Elmers, Saunders, Tombow)

Pages 34-35
Cutting tools

Trimmers (Carl, EK Success, Fiskars, Provo Craft, Tonic); decorative scissors, craft knives, shape cutter, rotary cutter (Fiskars); cutter (Tonic); blades (EK Success)

Page 36
Miscellaneous tools

Combination graphing/metal straightedge ruler (Creative Impressions); button shank remover (Blumenthal Lansing); tweezers (Making Memories); hammer; bone folder; eyelet setters; craft knife; pliers

Page 37
Pens

Pens (EK Success, Sakura of America, Staedtler)

Page 38
Good Times

Supplies: Letter template (EK Success); circle and flower template (Provo Craft); patterned papers (Autumn Leaves); rub-on words (Déjà Views); letter sticker (Doodlebug Design); paper flower (Prima); textured cardstock (Bazzill); brad

Page 38
Templates

Templates (Déjà Views, EK Success)

Page 39
Time in a Cone

Supplies: Nesting punches (EK Success); patterned paper, sticker punctuation (American Crafts); paper flower, brads (Chatterbox); chipboard letters (Pressed Petals); letter stickers (Doodlebug Design); rub-on word (Autumn Leaves); tag (Avery); textured cardstock (Bazzill)

Page 39
Punches

Nesting and corner punches (EK Success); hole punch (Fiskars)

Page 40
Photo Shoot Gone Bad

Supplies: Stickers and patterned papers (Sandylion); letter, decorative and corner brads (Queen & Co.); ribbon (May Arts, Offray); wooden tag (Chatterbox); photo hangers (Daisy D's); textured cardstock (Bazzill); leather ribbon

Page 40
Stickers

Cardstock stickers and letter stickers (Sandylion)

Page 41
Beautiful Child of Mine

Supplies: Rub-ons, patterned papers, coaster elements (Imagination Project); chipboard letters (Heidi Swapp); corner punch (EK Success); textured cardstock (Bazzill); distress ink (Ranger)

Page 41
Rub-ons

Rub-on letters and accents, patterned papers (Imagination Project)

Page 42
Die cuts

Die-cut machines, die cuts (Accu-Cut, Ellison, Sizzix, QuicKutz)

Page 43
Sweet Sister

Supplies: Die-cut flowers (Sizzix); die-cut eyelet letters (AccuCut); die-cut photo turns, letters (QuicKutz); die-cut buckles, decorative square (Spellbinders Paper Arts); die-cut chunky letters, label holder (Ellison); patterned papers (Chatterbox, Scenic Route Paper Co); flower brads (Making Memories); textured cardstock (Prism Papers); cardstock; stamping ink; vellum; foam spacers

Page 44
Bloom

Supplies: Letter and floral stamps (Hero Arts); patterned papers (Provo Craft); rub-on phrase (Basic Grey); photo turn (Boxer Scrapbook Productions); photo corners (Heidi Swapp); textured cardstock (Bazzill); stamping ink; brads

Page 44
Stamps

Stamps (Hero Arts, Technique Tuesday)

Page 46
Colorants

Colored crystal lacquers, 3D crystal lacquer (Sakura Hobby Craft); blending chalks (Plaid); decorating chalks, E-Z Chalk Enhancer (Craf-T Products); watercolor pencils (Staedtler); ink pads (Tsukineko); cat's eye ink pads (Clearsnap)

Page 49
Winner

Supplies: Acrylic letters, eyelet ribbon, mini brads (Junkitz); paper flowers, metal flower charm (Making Memories); label holder, photo turns, decorative brads (Queen & Co.); patterned papers (K & Company); corner punch (McGill); textured cardstock (Bazzill)

Pages 49-50
Embellishment How-To

Embellishments (Heidi Swapp, Junkitz, Prima, Queen & Co.)

Page 51
Premade page accents

Embellishments (Creative Imaginations, Me & My Big Ideas, Memories in the Making, Prima)

Page 52
4Ever

Supplies: Patterned papers (Basic Grey); ribbon (May Arts, Offray); photo corners (Heidi Swapp); epoxy heart, license plate, money clip, printed twill (Creative Imaginations); decorative photo corners, brads (Chatterbox)

Page 52
Page Accent Kits

Premade page accents (Chatterbox, Creative Imaginations)

Page 53
Premade page kits

Page kit (K & Company)

Pages 54-55

Patterned papers, rub-on words (Junkitz); die-cut machine

(QuicKutz); photo file box (MBI); paper trimmer, craft knife, paper-tear edger (Fiskars); adhesive runner (WeRMemoryKeepers); blending chalks (Plaid); embellishments (Queen & Co.)

Page 59
Paper selection based on photographs

Patterned papers (Imagination Project, Scenic Route Paper Co.); textured cardstocks (Prism Papers)

Page 60
Paper selection color theory and combinations

Color wheel (Memory Makers); patterned papers (Imagination Project, Junkitz, Sandylion, Scenic Route Paper Co.); textured cardstocks (Prism Papers)

Page 63
Kings & Queen

Supplies: Patterned papers (Scenic Route Paper Co.); chipboard letters (Heidi Swapp, Li'l Davis Designs); textured cardstock (Prism Papers); acrylic paint; transparency; Torrey Scott, Thornton, Colorado; Photos: Kelli Noto, Centennial Colorado

Page 64
A View to the Underwater World

Supplies: Patterned paper (Scenic Route Paper Co.); die-cut letters (QuicKutz); corner slot punch (EK Success); textured cardstock (Prism Papers); image-editing software (Adobe Photoshop Elements). Kelli Noto, Centennial, Colorado

Page 65
Primate House

Supplies: Patterned paper (Scenic Route Paper Co.); chipboard letter (Heidi Swapp); die-cut letters (QuicKutz); diamond punch (EK Success); textured cardstock (Prism Papers); transparency. Kelli Noto; Centennial, Colorado

Page 66
Polar Express

Supplies: Patterned papers (Scenic Route Paper Co.); letter template (Déjà Views); die-cut letters (Spellbinders Paper Arts); textured cardstock (Prism Papers); foam spacers. Torrey Scott, Thornton, Colorado; Photos: Kelli Noto, Centennial, Colorado

Page 67
Zoo in Review

Supplies: Patterned papers (Scenic Route Paper Co.); letter stickers (Bo-Bunny Press); decorative brads (Queen & Co.); textured cardstock (Prism Papers); stamping ink. Torrey Scott, Thornton, Colorado; Photos: Kelli Noto, Centennial, Colorado

Page 70
Matting ideas

Patterned papers (Scenic Route Paper Co.); ribbons (Li'l Davis Designs, Michaels, Offray); button; embroidery floss; brads; cardstock. Torrey Scott, Thornton, Colorado; Photos: Kelli Noto, Centennial, Colorado

Page 73
Title ideas

Patterned papers (Imagination Project, Scenic Route Paper Co.); die-cut letters (QuicKutz); ribbon (Offray); letter template (EK Success); foam stamps, mini brads (Making Memories); ransom letters (Autumn Leaves, Carolee's Creations, Creative Imaginations, EK Success, Junkitz, LazerLetterz, ScrapArts, SEI, Westrim); chalk; acrylic paint; pen; stamping ink. Torrey Scott, Thornton, Colorado

Page 75
Wild Things

Supplies: Patterned papers (Imagination Project, Scenic Route Paper Co.); coaster embellishments, rub-on letters (Imagination Project); die-cut letters (QuicKutz); textured cardstock (Prism Papers);

foam spacers; transparency; stamping ink. Kelli Noto, Centennial, Colorado

Pages 76-77

Album (Colorbök); patterned papers (Carolee's Creations); journaling notebook (source unknown); journaling pen (Staedtler)

Page 79

Patterned paper (Chatterbox); journaling pen (Staedtler)

Pages 80-81
Father & Son

Supplies: Patterned papers, wooden frame, photo corners, snaps (Chatterbox); die-cut shape (Spellbinders Paper Arts); die-cut letters (QuicKutz); textured cardstock (Bazzill)

Page 84
Precious

Supplies: Patterned papers, rub-on elements, ribbon (Autumn Leaves); index tab (Creative Imagination); plastic letters, flower silhouette (Heidi Swapp); journaling pen (EK Success); chalk (Craf-T); button; sequins; vintage trim

Page 85
Chalk Art

Supplies: Patterned papers (K & Company, KI Memories); ribbon (Making Memories); acrylic accent (KI Memories); chipboard letters (Heidi Swapp); photo turns (7 Gypsies); photo corners (Canson); hooks (Prym-Dritz); brads; cardstock

Page 86

Supplies: Patterned papers (KI Memories, Scenic Route Paper Co.); textured cardstocks (Prism Papers); journaling pen (Staedtler); foam adhesive

Page 87
A Peek Into Your Day

Supplies: Patterned papers (Junkitz, Me & My Big Ideas); photo turns, brads, safety pin (Junkitz); photo hanger (Daisy D's); chipboard letters (Heidi Swapp); letter stickers (Karen Foster Design, Li'l Davis Designs, Making Memories,); textured cardstock (Bazzill)

Page 88
Carefree Day

Supplies: Patterned papers (Bo-Bunny Press); colored brads (SEI); buckle (Junkitz); ribbon (Maya Road); punch (Marvy/Uchida); rub-on letters (Li'l Davis Designs); vellum; tag

Page 88
Tag

Supplies: Patterned paper (Junkitz); brads (Making Memories); ribbon (Creative Impressions); rickrack; cardstock

Page 89
Wild Eggs

Supplies: Patterned paper (Autumn Leaves); rub-on words (Déjà Views); rub-on stitches (K & Company); acrylic letters (Heidi Swapp); colored brads (Making Memories); epoxy letters (Li'l Davis Designs); paper hanger (Daisy D's); textured cardstock (Bazzill); buttons

Page 90
Fun

Supplies: Patterned papers (SEI); acrylic letters (Heidi Grace Designs); leather flower (Making Memories); textured cardstock (Bazzill); fabric; brad; stamping ink

Page 90
He

Supplies: Patterned paper, pillow flower, epoxy flower (Autumn Leaves); ribbon (Offray); letter stickers (American Crafts); textured cardstock (Bazzill); pen

Page 91
I Love This Puppy

Supplies: Patterned paper (7 Gypsies); ribbon (May Arts); label maker (Dymo); textured cardstock (Bazzill)

Page 92
Juice Cheeks

Supplies: Patterned papers, letter stickers (Arctic Frog); circle sticker (Scrapworks); tab sticker (Doodlebug Design); corner punch (Marvy/Uchida); opaque white pen (Sanford Corp.); textured cardstock (Bazzill); brad

Page 93
What's in a Name?

Supplies: Patterned paper (Chatterbox); chipboard punctuation (Heidi Swapp); chipboard heart (Making Memories); textured cardstock (Bazzill)

Page 93
Sophie

Supplies: Patterned papers (Carolee's Creations, Creative Imaginations, Rusty Pickle); epoxy words, stencil letters, metal charms and frames (Li'l Davis Designs); epoxy letters (K & Company, Li'l Davis Designs); textured cardstock (Bazzill); date stamp (Making Memories); woven label (Me & My Big Ideas); letter stamps (Hero Arts, PSX Design); stamping ink

Page 94
Sk8tr Boy

Supplies: Textured cardstock (Die Cuts with a View, Prism Papers); die-cut letters (A2Z Essentials); chipboard stars (Heidi Swapp); letter stickers (American Crafts, Scrapworks); circle punch (EK Success); staples; cardstock; foam tape

Page 94
Talk

Supplies: Patterned paper (Imagination Project); chipboard letters (Zsiage); corner punch (EK Success); textured cardstock (Bazzill); pen

Page 95
Brothers

Supplies: Patterned papers (KI Memories); rub ons (Making Memories); clay letters (Li'l Davis Designs); textured cardstock (Bazzill)

Pages 96-97

Patterned papers, word and letter stickers, ribbons (Carolee's Creations); album, adhesive dispenser (We R Memory Keepers); photo case (ArtBin); scissors (Fiskars); mini paper trimmer (EK Success); paper flower (Prima)

Pages 98-99
Baby Love Album

Supplies: 8 x 8" album (Westrim); patterned papers; letter stickers (SEI); chipboard letters (Heidi Swapp); tags, ribbons (Making Memories); rub-ons (KI Memories); chipboard hearts (Heidi Swapp, Making Memories); Photos: Shelley Rassenfoss, Shelbyville, Kentucky

Pages 100-101
S Album

Supplies: 8 x 8" album (Westrim); letter stickers, brads, ribbon, metal letter (American Crafts); sequin flowers, letter brad, decorative brad (Queen & Co.); fabric paper (Michael Miller Memories); frame (Li'l Davis Designs); gaffer tape (7 Gypsies); specialty paper (Sakar Papers); circle punch (Marvy/Uchida); photo corners (Heidi Swapp); rub-on letters (Making Memories); textured cardstocks (WorldWin); stamping ink; Photo of Susan as adult by: Nisa Fiin of Shooting Stars Portraits, St. Paul, Minnesota

Pages 102-103
Love That Dog Album

Supplies: Album (American Traditional Designs); patterned papers, twill accents (Carolee's Creations); frame, plaque (Little Black Dress Designs); die-cut letters, shape (QuicKutz); rub-on accents

(Carolee's Creations, Memories Complete); textured cardstock (Bazzill); stamping ink

Pages 104-105
Our Wedding Album

Supplies: 8 x 8" album (Colorbök); patterned papers, acrylic hearts (Heidi Grace Designs); paper flowers (Prima); ribbons (Michaels, Offray); decorative brads, acrylic tags, sequin flower accents (Queen & Co.); textured cardstock (Bazzill)

Page 106
Christmas Album

Supplies: Album (Scrap Artistry); decorative scissors (Fiskars); premade page accents (EK Success); cardstock

Pages 107-108
The album-making process

Patterned papers (Imagination Project); ribbon (Offray); conchos (Scrapworks); metal-rimmed tags, word slides (American Crafts); vacation word plates (Making Memories); architectural brads (K & Company); paper charms (Pebbles); travel stickers (Creative Imaginations, S.R.M. Press, Sticker Studio); word stickers (Colorbök, Making Memories, Me & My Big Ideas); tree brads (Creative Impressions); pen (Staedtler); album (Colorbök); paper trimmer (Tonic); scissors (Fiskars); adhesive runner (We R Memory Keepers); cardstock; clips

Page 109
Green Eyes/Animal Lover

Supplies: Patterned papers (K & Company); letter stickers, brads (Making Memories); rub-on letters (Imagination Project); buttons (Autumn Leaves); die-cut photo turn (Sizzix); die-cut photo corner (QuicKutz); ribbon (American Crafts); cardstock

Page 110
Hawaii Album

Supplies: Patterned papers (Me & My Big Ideas); letter stickers (Bo-Bunny Press); rub-on letters (Imagination Project); ribbon (American Crafts); flowers, brads (Making Memories); textured cardstock (Bazzill); tags

Page 111
Christmas Greetings Album

Supplies: Spiral album (Heidi Swapp); leather flowers, decorative brads, metal charms, ribbon, lace (Making Memories); patterned papers, rub-ons, stickers, tags, library card (Daisy D's); ribbon, safety pin (Li'l Davis Designs); letter stickers (Basic Grey); fibers (Bazzill); gel pen (Sanford Corp.)

Page 113
Official Beach Bums

Supplies: Glass bottles (www.scrapps.net); patterned papers (Creative Imaginations); stickers (Bo-Bunny Press, Creative Imaginations); monogram letter (My Mind's Eye); transparency; stamping ink; jute; ribbon

Page 113
Memorabilia

Supplies: 3D Keepers (Déjà Views); keepsake pockets (Fiskars)

Page 114
Celebrate!

Supplies: Patterned papers (Scenic Route Paper Co.); ribbons (May Arts, Offray); rub-on letters (K & Company.); textured cardstock (Bazzill); staples; stamping ink

Page 115
Homemade Page Kits

Double pocket page protector (Cropper Hopper); patterned papers, page accents (My Mind's Eye); metal embellishments (Nunn Design)

Pages 116-117

Monitor and keyboard (Hewlett Packard); albums (Colorbök); organizer boxes (MBI); scissors, craft knife (Fiskars); floral list, self-stick notes (Innovative Storage Designs); pens (Staedtler)

Pages 118-119

Photos courtesy of Cut 'n Paste, Boise, Idaho and Scrapbook Retailer magazine.

Page 121
Conventions and scrapbook shows

Supplies: Ribbon (Offray); slot punch (Family Treasures); cardstock; thread; Photos: Dian Carville, Dallas, Texas

Page 122
Aloha

Supplies: Patterned papers (SEI); letter stamps, brads (Making Memories); ribbon (Offray); acrylic flowers (KI Memories); textured cardstock (Bazzill); acrylic paint; silk flower; stamping ink

Page 123

Photo tote and cases (ArtBin); scrapbook organizer (Crop In Style); mini cutter (EK Success); adhesive runner (We R Memory Keepers); paper flower (Prima); page accents (Carolee's Creations); craft knife, scissors (Fiskars); ruler (C-Thru Ruler)

Page 125
Swaps

Supplies: Heart punch (Punch Bunch); pens, tag stamp (EK Success)

Page 126
X-Static

Supplies: Patterned papers (Close To My Heart, Doodlebug Design, Provo Craft); textured cardstock (Prism Papers); die-cut letters (QuicKutz)

Page 126
X-Static Revised

Supplies: Patterned papers (Close to My Heart, Doodlebug Design, Provo Craft); colored brads (Making Memories); chipboard letters (Li'l Davis Designs); textured cardstock (Prism Papers)

Page 127
Mail-order clubs

Club kit (Club Scrap)

Sources

The following companies manufacture products featured in this book. Please check your local retailers to find these materials, or go to a company's Web site for the latest product. In addition, we have made every attempt to properly credit the items mentioned in this book. We apologize to any company that we have listed incorrectly, and we would appreciate hearing from you.

3L Corporation
(800) 828-3130
www.scrapbook-adhesives.com

3M
(800) 364-3577
www.3m.com

7 Gypsies
(877) 749-7797
www.sevengypsies.com

A2Z Essentials
(419) 663-2869
www.a2zessentials.com

AccuCut®
(800) 288-1670
www.accucut.com

Adobe Systems Incorporated
(866) 766-2256
www.adobe.com

Advantus Corp.
(904) 482-0091
www.advantus.com

American Crafts
(801) 226-0747
www.americancrafts.com

American Traditional Designs®
(800) 448-6656
www.americantraditional.com

Arctic Frog
(479) 636-FROG
www.arcticfrog.com

ArtBin (a division of
Flambeau, Inc.)
(800) 457-5252
www.flambeau.com

Artograph, Inc.
(888) 975-9555
www.artograph.com

Autumn Leaves
(800) 588-6707
www.autumnleaves.com

Avery Dennison Corporation
(800) GO-AVERY
www.avery.com

Basic Grey™
(801) 451-6006
www.basicgrey.com

Bazzill Basics Paper
(480) 558-8557
www.bazzillbasics.com

Beacon Adhesives
(800) 865-7238

Berwick Offray™, LLC
(800) 344-5533
www.offray.com

Big Time Products, LLC
(formerly un-du)
(888) Buy-undu
www.un-du.com

Blumenthal Lansing Company
(201) 935-6220
www.buttonsplus.com

Bo-Bunny Press
(801) 771-4010
www.bobunny.com

Boxer Scrapbook Productions
(503) 625-0455
www.boxerscrapbooks.com

Canson®, Inc.
(800) 628-9283
www.canson-us.com

CARL Mfg. USA, Inc.
(800) 257-4771
www.Carl-Products.com

Carolee's Creations®
(435) 563-1100
www.ccpaper.com

Chatterbox, Inc.
(208) 939-9133
www.chatterboxinc.com

Clearsnap, Inc.
(360) 293-6634
www.clearsnap.com

Close To My Heart®
(888) 655-6552
www.closetomyheart.com

Club Scrap™, Inc.
(888) 634-9100
www.clubscrap.com

Colorbök™, Inc.
(800) 366-4660
www.colorbok.com

Craf-T Products
(507) 235-3996
www.craf-tproducts.com

Creative Imaginations
(800) 942-6487
www.cigift.com

Creative Impressions Rubber
Stamps, Inc.
(719) 596-4860
www.creativeimpressions.com

C.R. Gibson®
(800) 243-6004
www.crgibson.com

Crop In Style®
(888) 700-2202
www.cropinstyle.com

Cropper Hopper™/Advantus
Corporation
(800) 826-8806
www.cropperhopper.com

C-Thru® Ruler Company, The
(800) 243-8419
www.cthruruler.com

Daisy D's Paper Company
(888) 601-8955
www.daisydspaper.com

Dèjá Views
(800) 243-8419
www.dejaviews.com

Die Cuts With A View
(801) 224-6766
www.diecutswithaview.com

DMD Industries, Inc.
(800) 805-9890
www.dmdind.com

Doodlebug Design™ Inc.
(801) 966-9952
www.doodlebug.ws

Dymo
(800) 426-7827
www.dymo.com

Eastman Kodak Company
(770) 522-2542
www.kodak.com

EK Success™, Ltd.
(800) 524-1349
www.eksuccess.com

Ellison®
(800) 253-2238
www.ellison.com

Elmer's Products, Inc.
(614) 225-4000
www.elmers.com

Epson America, Inc.
(562) 981-3840
www.epson.com

Family Treasures®
(949) 290-0872
www.familytreasures.com

Fiskars®, Inc.
(800) 950-0203
www.fiskars.com

Generations
(800) 905-1888
www.generationsnow.com

Handbags Full of Memories
(787) 612-0500
www.handbagsfullofmemories.
com

Heidi Grace Designs, Inc.
(608) 294-4509
www.heidigrace.com

Heidi Swapp/Advantus Corporation
(904) 482-0092
www.heidiswapp.com

Hero Arts® Rubber Stamps, Inc.
(800) 822-4376
www.heroarts.com

Hewlett-Packard Company
www.hp.com/go/scrapbooking

Highsmith, Inc.
(800) 554-4661
www.highsmith.com

Hunt Corporation
(800) 879-4868
www.hunt-corp.com

Imagination Project, Inc.
(513) 860-2711
www.imaginationproject.com

Innovative Storage Designs, Inc.
(262) 241-3749
www.innovative-storage.com

Junkitz™
(732) 792-1108
www.junkitz.com

K & Company
(888) 244-2083
www.kandcompany.com

Karen Foster Design
(801) 451-9779
www.karenfosterdesign.com

KI Memories
(972) 243-5595
www.kimemories.com

Konica Minolta Photo Imaging
U.S.A., Inc.
(800) 285-6422
www.konicaminolta.com

Krylon®
(216) 566-200
www.krylon.com

LazerLetterz
(281) 627-4227
www.lazerletterz.com

Light Impressions®
(800) 828-6216
www.lightimpressionsdirect.
com

Li'l Davis Designs
(949) 838-0344
www.lildavisdesigns.com

Little Black Dress Designs
(360) 894-8844
www.littleblackdressdesigns.
com

Making Memories
(800) 286-5263
www.makingmemories.com

Marvy® Uchida/ Uchida of
America, Corp.
(800) 541-5877
www.uchida.com

Maya Road, LLC
(214) 488-3279
www.mayaroad.com

May Arts
(800) 442-3950
www.mayarts.com

MBI/MCS Industries, Inc.
(847) 749-0225
www.mcsframes.com

McGill, Inc.
(800) 982-9884
www.mcgillinc.com

me & my BiG ideas®
(949) 883-2065
www.meandmybigideas.com

Memories Complete™, LLC
(866) 966-6365
www.memoriescomplete.com

Memories in the Making/
Leisure Arts
(800) 643-8030
www.leisurearts.com

Michael Miller Memories
(212) 704-0774
www.michaelmillermemories.
com

Michaels® Arts & Crafts
(800) 642-4235
www.michaels.com

My Mind's Eye™, Inc.
(800) 665-5116
www.frame-ups.com

Novelcrafts
(541) 582-3208
www.novelcrafts.com

Nunn Design
(360) 379-3557
www.nunndesign.com

Offray- see Berwick Offray, LLC

Pebbles Inc.
(801) 224-1857
www.pebblesinc.com

Photographic Solutions, Inc.
(508) 759-2322
www.photosol.com

Plaid Enterprises, Inc.
(800) 842-4197
www.plaidonline.com

Pressed Petals
(800) 748-4656
www.pressedpetals.com

Prima Marketing, Inc.
(909) 627-5532
www.mulberrypaperflowers.
com

Print File®, Inc.
(800) 508-8539
www.printfile.com

Prism™ Papers
(866) 902-1002
www.prismpapers.com

Provo Craft®
(888) 577-3545
www.provocraft.com

Prym-Dritz Corporation
www.dritz.com

PSX Design™
(800) 782-6748
www.psxdesign.com

Punch Bunch, The
(254) 791-4209
www.thepunchbunch.com

Queen & Co.
(858) 485-5132
www.queenandcompany.com

QuicKutz, Inc.
(801) 765-1144
www.quickutz.com

Ranger Industries, Inc.
(800) 244-2211
www.rangerink.com

Rusty Pickle
(801) 746-1045
www.rustypickle.com

S.R.M. Press, Inc.
(800) 323-9589
www.srmpress.com

Sakar Papers
(888) 400-9768
www.sakarpapers.com

Sakura Hobby Craft
(310) 212-7878
www.sakuracraft.com

Sakura of America
(800) 776-6257
www.sakuraofamerica.com

Sandylion Sticker Designs
(800) 387-4215
www.sandylion.com

Sanford® Corporation
(800) 323-0749
www.sanfordcorp.com

Saunders
(207) 685-3385
www.saunders-usa.com

Scenic Route Paper Co.
(801) 785-0761
www.scenicroutepaper.com

Scrap Artistry
(860) 521-5926
www.scrapartistry.com

ScrapArts
(503) 631-4893
www.scraparts.com

Scrapworks, LLC
(801) 363-1010
www.scrapworks.com

SEI, Inc.
(800) 333-3279
www.shopsei.com

Sizzix®
(866) 742-4447
www.sizzix.com

Smead
(651) 437-4111
www.smead.com

Spellbinders™ Paper Arts, LLC
(888) 547-0400
www.spellbinders.us

Staedtler®, Inc.
(800) 927-7723
www.staedtler.us

Sticker Studio™
(208) 322-2465
www.stickerstudio.com

Technique Tuesday, LLC
(503) 644-4073
www.techniquetuesday.com

Therm O Web, Inc.
(800) 323-0799
www.thermoweb.com

Tombow®
(800) 835-3232
www.tombowusa.com

Tonic® Studios USA, Inc.
(608) 836-4478
www.kushgrip.com

Tsukineko®, Inc.
(800) 769-6633
www.tsukineko.com

We R Memory Keepers, Inc.
(801) 539-5000
www.weronthenet.com

Westrim® Crafts
(800) 727-2727
www.westrimcrafts.com

WorldWin Paper
(888) 843-6455
www.thepapermill.com

Xyron
(800) 793-3523
www.xyron.com

Zsiage, LLC
(718) 224-1976
www.zsiage.com

Index

A

Achieve album continuity design using a variety of patterned papers, 110

Acrostic journaling, 95

Add page accents, 57

Add title and journaling, 57

Adding a title, 72

Adding journaling, 74

Adding lacquer shine, 47

Adding page accents, 74

Additional instructions & credits, 132-137

Additional tools for your supply box, 36

Adhering page accents, 33

Album bindings, 29

Album-making process, The, 107

Albums, 28

Applying chalk, 46

Applying inked definition, 47

Assembling the page, 71

Attaching acrylics, 49

Attaching metallics, 50

Attaching other accents, 50

Attaching ribbon, 50

B

Baby album, 98

Balance, 65

Basic toolbox, The, 26

Becoming a club member, 127

Become a photo detective, 82

Becoming a savvy scrapbooking shopper, 119

Bindings, 29

Book clubs, 127

Burning and sharing images, 23

C

Cardstock, patterned and specialty papers, 30

Carry continuity through album with imagery and journaling, 111

Character-study journaling, 79

Character-traits journaling, 90

Choosing an album, 108

Choosing papers, 59

Christmas album, 106

Chronological albums, 98

Classes, 118

Color copier, 20

Colorant how-to, 47

Colorant types, 46

Colorants, 46

Coloring a stamp, 45

Common themes for sorting photos, 15

Completing the page's design, 74

Conducting an interview, 83

Connecting in the Scrapbook World, 116-127

Consider layout and design, 56

Consumable vs. non-consumable supplies, 26

Conventions, 121

Conversational journaling, 94

Craft knives, 34

Creating a card or worksheet for each year, 11

Creating a stamped image, 45

Creating album continuity, 109

Creating continuity on page spreads, 67

Creating letter-sticker titles, 72

Creating Your First Scrapbook Album, 96-115

Critique groups, 126

Crop photos, 57

Cropped, enlarged photo, 68

Cropping for visual interest, 68

Cropping group page, 122

Cropping kit, 123

Cropping on-the-go, 123

Cropping photos, 68

Crops, 122

Cutting tools, 34

D

De-acidifying memorabilia, 19

Decorative pens, 37

Decorative scissors, 35

Decorative-pen results, 37

Descriptive journaling, 93

Designing computer-printed titles, 72

Designing with color, 60

Designing with patterns, 61

Designing Your First Scrapbook Page, 54-75

Determine focal photo, 56, 58

Die cuts, 42

Die-cut machine options, 42

Die-cut machines, 42

Die-cut page, 43

Digital photo machine, 20

Discovering the Joy of Journaling, 76-95

Distressed frame, 70

Do you already own these tools?, 27

Drop, crop and flop, 68

Dry adhesives, 32

E

Effective journaling, 81

Embellished page, 49, 52

Embellishment how-to, 49, 50

Embellishment varieties, 48

Embellishments, 48

Emotion journaling, 79

Encapsulating memorabilia, 19, 113

Engaging close-up; no cropping needed, 68

Ensuring unity throughout a theme album, 109

Event journaling, 78

F

Favorites journaling, 92

Finding a crop group, 122

Finding scrapbook-related titles at libraries and bookstores, 120

Finished page, The, 75

Focal point, 64

Folding memorabilia pocket edges, 114

Fold-out page, 87

G

Gathering the facts behind your photos, 82

Getting organized for a crop, 123

Getting the most out of scrapbooking classes, 118

Glossary of scrapbook terms, 128-133

Grids or sketches, 62